There were five of them. They stood between me and the door of the church vestry, pointing their rifles at my face. Their own faces were scarred with the distinctive tribal cuttings of the Kakwa tribe. They were dressed casually in flowered shirts and bell-bottom pants, and wore sunglasses. Although I had never seen any of them before, I recognized them immediately. They were the secret police of the State Research Bureau—Amin's Nubian assassins.

For a long moment no one said anything. Then the tallest man, obviously the leader, spoke. "We are going to kill you," he said. "If you have something to say, say it before you die."

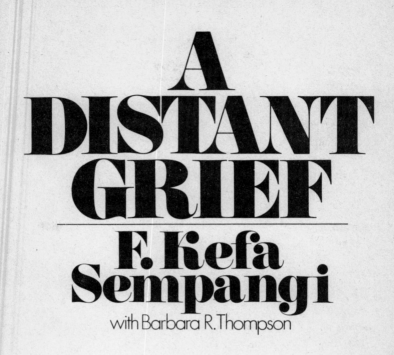

A DISTANT GRIEF

F. Kefa Sempangi

with Barbara R. Thompson

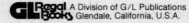

GL Regal Books A Division of G/L Publications
Glendale, California, U.S.A.

Other good Regal reading:
Peace Child, by Don Richardson
Lords of the Earth, by Don Richardson
Autobiography of God, by Lloyd John Ogilvie

The foreign language publishing of all Regal books is under the direction of GLINT. GLINT provides financial and technical help for the adaptation, translation and publishing of books in more than 85 languages for millions of people worldwide.

For more information write: GLINT, 110 W. Broadway, Glendale, CA 91204.

Scripture quotations in this publication are from the Authorized King James Version and the *RSV, Revised Standard Version* of the Bible, copyrighted 1946 and 1952 by the Division of Christian Education of the NCCC, U.S.A., and used by permission.

Second Printing, 1979

Published by Regal Books Division, G/L Publications
Glendale, California 91209
Printed in U.S.A.

Library of Congress Catalog Card No. 79-50394
Soft-cover edition: ISBN 0-8307-0684-4
Hardcover edition: ISBN 0-8307-0691-7

To my departed mother Lovinsa Nakazibwe, for her vision in getting me to school—to read the Bible to her.

I want to express my gratitude to Barbara Thompson for her willingness, patience and commitment. We can both look at this book as a finished product of God's grace. It is a commendable thing for Barbara to step over the cross-cultural line and identify with a stranger and write the book with me.

Contents

Foreword

In that moment I learned a new truth. I learned that just as there is a boundary beyond which human beings cannot comprehend the glory of God, so there is a boundary beyond which they cannot comprehend the evil in the world. There is a boundary beyond which everything is a senseless chasm. It is here in the nightmare of utter chaos that human feeling dies. It is here, where death and terror seem to have full dominion, that even the deepest sorrow becomes but a distant grief.

—F. Kefa Sempangi

Reading this compelling record of faith versus atrocity in three sittings during a brief holiday was a profound spiritual experience which will not soon be forgotten.

One reads with unbelief this record of the reign of terror orchestrated by Idi Amin, an unbelief incidentally, apparently characteristic of much of the outside world which dismissed Amin as "an international buffoon whose strange exploits bemused the civilized world." The truth in this instance was simply beyond the boundary of human comprehension.

To the glory of God the indescribable brutality of Amin's soldiers and his hired Nubian assassins was no match for the stubborn courage and faith of the Christians. Some of the most inhumane capitulated to Christ because of the glowing triumph of the Ugandan believers. Often while reading I was reminded of Jesus's word to His disciples, "I send you forth as sheep in the midst of wolves."

The contradiction of "normalcy" and idiocy is unreal: business as usual, dignified homes midst expansive gardens in affluent neighborhoods, golfers enjoying their rounds on sun-drenched courses, young couples strolling meadowed slopes—against the capricious madness and mindlessness of a completely unpredictable leader.

It seemed impossible that believers could endure, yet the explosive expansion of the church witnesses to the fact that against that which Christ is building, "the gates of hell shall not prevail."

This book tells the story of the quiet heroism of believers whose strength and resilience lay in "walking in the light." They took their relationships with Christ and one another seriously. They refused to allow sin to alienate by being quick to confess and forgive. They loved and cared freely and selflessly. ". . . there is nothing you can repay. Perhaps you are thinking now that giving is a two-way street but to tell the truth it is a flowing river. It does not stop or return but only passes on."

Their faithfulness despite inconceivably dehumanizing circumstances, the relentless thread of ruthless and insatiable brutality and imminent unexpected betrayal is a modern counterpart to Hebrews chapter eleven.

This record demonstrates the biblical truth so often manifested through church history that the people of God are pilgrims and aliens in a world ruled by the rapacious god of deceit, intrigue, and murder—Satan. The frighteningly contemporary events in Uganda argue for this reality and warn all believers to beware the delusion of a status quo, this-worldly life-style. Comfortable conformity to the world in which we live today may be the most subtle form of Christ denial.

Richard C. Halverson

—Richard C. Halverson

Preface

The student shifted his weight from one foot to the next as he stood in front of my desk. It was an awkward moment for both of us. He was a bright, capable young man but in the last weeks his performance in class had fallen far below average. His last exam was unreadable and, against my will, I gave him a failing grade.

Now I held the exam in my hand as evidence and tried to challenge the boy to work harder. He only stared at me vacantly. When I finished speaking there was a long silence of several minutes before he spoke.

"I will try to work harder, Professor Sempangi."

He said the words without conviction and walked away. At the door he turned suddenly and his face was no longer empty but furious.

"Not long ago Idi Amin's soldiers came through my village," he said, his voice full of a remembered grief.

"Now my father is buried, my mother is dead with a terrible death, and my brother has disappeared. I have no home and I can hardly find food. And I am not alone. Our whole country is in desolation. Amin's victims are everywhere. They are lying unburied in the streets and in the forests, and they are rotting before heaven. But where is God? Is He dead? How could He exist and tolerate this evil?"

It was October, 1972, and I was lecturing in art history at Makerere University in Uganda. Uganda, once described by Winston Churchill as "the Pearl of Africa," was celebrating its tenth anniversary since independence—in blood. While the western world dismissed stories of genocide as wild exaggerations, Idi Amin had systematically exterminated 90,000 people in three months. In a few short years Uganda's death toll would stand at over 300,000 and all hope for rescue would be dead. *The New York Times* would report:

> *Nearly 30 years after the foundation of the United Nations, there is still no mechanism to protect citizens from the arbitrary madness of governments; mass murder in Uganda and elsewhere remains, for the United Nations and the United States government, a distant grief at best.[1]*

From the beginning the primary target of Amin's brutality was the Christian church. All of his victims suffered unspeakably. They were tortured and humiliated in front of families and friends. They were dismembered, decapitated, made to eat their own flesh. Their bodies were fed to crocodiles or left unburied in streets and forests. Perhaps worst of all, an entire generation of Ugandan children was growing up having known nothing but suffering and terror.

In this atmosphere the question raised by my bright, failing student was not a distant intellectual problem. It was not the *problem* of evil which troubled him. It was the *presence* of evil, its physical invasion into his life. Two thousand years ago the Jews might have asked: If God is alive, why is John the Baptist dead and Herod Antipas still living? Now, this student asked the same question: If God is alive, why are thousands of His children murdered and Idi Amin still living?

Six years later his question still rings in my mind. This book has been written as a belated reply. It is not written to provide an intellectual answer to the terrible problem of evil in the world. It is written only to witness to God's answer to the suffering and terror taking place in one small country on the African continent. It is written to witness to God's presence in Uganda.

In part this story is my story and the story of my family. In part it is the story of General Idi Amin—one cannot tell the story of God's people in Egypt without speaking of the Pharaoh who oppressed them. But most of all it is the story of the church, God's people, those called apart to witness to the presence of God's Kingdom in the midst of genocide and terror. It is these men and women, and thousands of others like them around the globe, whose task it is to stand with God against the powers of evil which grip the world. It is these men and women against whom, God has promised, even the gates of hell will not prevail.

F. Kefa Sempangi

F. Kefa Sempangi
December, 1978

1

The Fugitive Woman

Walala, walala, tulaba kuki! "Whom do we see?"
O kabula da! "You who have been lost for ages!"
It was early evening, in June of 1971. My wife Penina
and I had just arrived at a dinner party given by her
brother to celebrate our marriage and our return to
Uganda, our East African homeland.

Penina and I had been married in England in the
summer of 1968. At that time I was a graduate student
studying on a government grant at the Royal College of
Art in London. Penina, whom I had met in my home
church in Uganda, was just finishing advanced nurse's
training in Birmingham. My own studies were complet-
ed two years later and, at the invitation of Dr. Hans
Rookmaaker of Holland, Penina and I spent a year at
the Free University in Amsterdam.

We were in Amsterdam when we heard the news of Uganda's liberation. President Milton Obote had been overthrown. Since independence in 1962 President Obote had thrown hundreds of my tribe, the southern Baganda, into prison. By January of 1971 over 4,000 political prisoners crowded the jails of Kampala, Uganda's capital city. As one by one the men who could have stood against Obote's oppressive regime were imprisoned, all hope for justice disappeared.

It was then that freedom came. On January 25, a high-ranking army officer, General Idi Amin, led the Ugandan army in a successful *coup d'etat*. A short time later Radio Uganda announced that Obote and his followers had fled to Tanzania and General Amin had been asked by the armed forces to lead the country. Almost overnight, Amin became "the champion of liberty"; the golden days of Uganda had begun.

Now, on this warm June evening, Penina and I felt jubilation in our hearts. We were glad to be home and we were ready to begin a new life in the new Uganda. Penina's brother, Godfrey Lule, met us on the front steps of his home and our reunion was a most joyous occasion.

"My brother and sister!" Godfrey exclaimed as he embraced us warmly. "Welcome home to the freedom country!"

Godfrey's party was held in the front garden of his western-style Kampala home. By the time Penina and I arrived many distinguished guests were already gathered, mingling together around elegantly set tables or strolling along graveled paths lined with lush tropical plants. Godfrey was a well-known lawyer and the permanent secretary for the Ministry of Justice. His house was located in Kampala's most exclusive district and his friends were from the highest circles of Ugandan society. None of them wore traditional robes. The men were dressed in dark tailor-made suits and the women wore colorful, expensive gowns from Europe. In language and gesture everyone gave the appearance of cultured sophistication. *These exclusive people*, I thought to myself as I stared enviously around the garden, *are the Africans of tomorrow. They are Uganda's future.*

We sat down to eat, and the smell of curry was thick in the air. Table after table was piled high with the best traditional dishes. There was *matooke*, a dish of steamed bananas with a tomato and peanut sauce, and there were steamed and fried sweet potatoes. There were greens, goat, chicken, pork and beef, and a lavish selection of tropical fruits. In the background a stereo was playing the new music, a mixture of western guitars and African drums.

Godfrey's guests were mostly lawyers like himself and when the conversation turned to politics they spoke with confidence and deep optimism. Many of them had suffered under Obote's tyrannical regime and now, for the first time since independence, they had hope for themselves and hope for Uganda. The country's economic situation was improving steadily and all political prisoners had been released. General Amin, "the gentle, jolly giant," promised that military rule was only a temporary resting place on the road to freedom. In a few short years there would be a free and fair general election.

Amin was still making major political appointments and many of Godfrey's guests could expect prestigious positions in the new government. They joked among themselves and speculated in a friendly fashion about who would be the next to "fall into things," the expression used to describe someone's coming to power and wealth without effort. Amin himself had fallen into something. He was not a politician, nor was he educated. He was only an illiterate army man who was now the head of an entire country. Good fortune could come to anyone now.

I heard an undercurrent of opportunism in these discussions but I immediately excused it. This is not an upper class but a class in the making, I said to myself. It is a class of professional optimism. They will dream their dreams and together they will climb high on the tree of success. For a moment I had my own dream. I would climb higher than the lawyers. There was nothing standing in my way. I could be anything I wanted to be in the new Uganda. With a graduate degree from London and a new teaching position in Uganda's only university, the University of Makerere, I had all the credentials for success. All I needed was determination.

Penina and I left Godfrey's party late that evening and we both felt a strong optimism for our future. Within a few days Penina began work as a nurse at one of Kampala's largest hospitals and I started my teaching career in art history. In my first few weeks on Makerere Hill all my ambitions were fulfilled. I had a prestigious position, a good salary, a big house and a new car. My colleagues admired my paintings and my sculptures. Students, eager to hear western ideas from an artist with a British degree, crowded into my classroom. There were seldom empty seats and latecomers often had to sit in windows or stand in the doorway.

My greatest challenge came in the classroom as I tried to bring together my work in art history with my commitment to following Jesus Christ. I had become a Christian in 1961, as a young high school student, through the influence of a devout woman from the East African Revival Fellowship.[2] Immediately after my conversion I began working with local missionary organizations as an interpreter and part-time preacher for street evangelism programs. In this work of the church I was very zealous, but even after enrolling in Makerere University I had little understanding of how to bring my faith and my education together. It was not until after I left Uganda and met Dr. Hans Rookmaaker that I came to understand the intellectual framework of Christian belief. Now I was eager to share these insights with students. Word spread quickly among them that there was a Christian professor on the faculty and before long a steady stream of visitors came to my office door. Penina and I began a student Bible study in our home and much of my energy was spent in counseling. These discussions with students were challenging and rewarding, and often lasted late into the night.

My honeymoon experience with university life ended on a warm Sunday afternoon only a month after it began. Penina and I had gone to church that morning at the mission where I once worked as an interpreter. When the service was over, we mingled in the courtyard to greet old friends. With a bright equatorial sun burning in the sky it was a most joyous occasion, and dozens of children were laughing and shouting all around us.

We said our last good-bye and were turning our faces toward home when we heard another familiar greeting. We turned and were astonished to find standing before us "the fugitive woman." Penina and I had had a passing acquaintance with this homeless mother of three for many years, but had not seen her since we left for our studies in England. Strangely enough, while traveling one summer in North America, we saw her photograph many times.

The summer after we were married we made a trip to Canada to visit the home congregations of missionaries we had known in Uganda. As we went from church to church we were surprised to find a picture of the fugitive woman tacked on every missions bulletin board. She was dressed in her familiar rags, and at her side were her three small children wearing only dirty pieces of calico. Beneath her picture were boxes piled high with clothes. Penina and I were overwhelmed by the open-hearted generosity of church members who were giving with genuine love to a stranger. We rejoiced for the good fortune that had come to the fugitive woman.

Now, on this Sunday afternoon, the fugitive woman hurried toward us and embraced us as a mother receives her children. Her three small daughters stood close beside her and looked at us with shy faces.

Penina and I stared at the fugitive woman in astonishment. She was barefoot and wearing the same ragged dress we had seen in the photograph. Her children were more destitute than ever. They were dressed in torn and dirty rags. Running sores covered their legs, their stomachs were bloated and their hair was gray with malnutrition.

I could not take my eyes from the children. From far away I heard Penina make an angry noise. "Who is the father of these children?" she demanded indignantly.

The fugitive woman answered quickly. The joy of welcome still shone from her face and her voice was full of hope. "These are Jesus' children," she said.

With these words Penina burst into tears and in a few moments the fugitive woman was weeping with her. My own tears could not be controlled. The three little girls pressed close to their mother and stared at us silently. They did not know that we cried for them.

A few minutes later we said good-bye to the fugitive woman and went home to our Sunday dinner, but that evening as I lay on my comfortable bed, I could not sleep. The face of the fugitive woman was still fresh in my mind. I wondered where she was sleeping and if she had found a porch for the children. I thought of the bedroom reserved for our own unborn child. It was full of presents we had received from friends in Holland and there was already a crib set up in the corner. Our child would never need to sleep on the ground or on a stranger's front porch. She would dress well and never go hungry. What made her different from the children of the fugitive woman? What was special about Penina and me that was not special about their mother? Weren't we all children of faith, sons and daughters of Abraham? Yet the fugitive family dressed in rags while we wore fine garments. They ate the crumbs meant for dogs while we ate bread from the Father's table.

I thought of the photograph we had seen in Canada. Hadn't there been boxes beneath it piled high with donations? Who was eating the food and wearing the clothes intended for the fugitive family? Why had her suffering been used as an advertisement to raise funds for others? These questions came again and again to my mind, and I lay awake the rest of the night without peace and without understanding.

The next morning I went to the mission and paid a visit to the administrator in charge of distributing resources. I told him about my experiences in Canada and in the churchyard. "The fugitive woman receives nothing from you," I said. "Her picture is used, but she is not remembered."

The man shrugged his shoulders. There was nothing to be done. "You have been gone too long," he said. "You have forgotten the problems we face. We see thousands of starving and ragged children every day. You see them yourself. You know we can't help everyone. The woman of whom you speak knows the Lord and is happy. Her reward will come."

I left the mission office and walked home with many questions racing through my head. *Why doesn't this man react?* I asked myself. *Is he immune from suffering? Can't he see beyond the barriers of his comfortable life? His own family eats well. His own family has good clothes to wear. They sleep in the safety of the mission compound. How can he tell the fugitive woman her reward is in heaven when his own is on earth?*

As my heart burned against the man at the mission I heard the convicting voice of God. How could I take a speck from my brother's eye when there was a beam in my own? Was there something to be said about him that could not be said about me? I had seen the fugitive woman in the streets since I was a student at the University of Makerere. I had passed her on the way to class and from a distance I called her sister. Once I even shared a passage of Scripture with her, and she had memorized a dozen verses without effort. At that moment I had admired her intelligence and been touched by her sincere faith. But never once had I been touched by her poverty. I had never shed tears for her children— the comfort of my academic life had insulated me from her need.

As the face of the fugitive woman floated before me I saw in my mind the faces of two children I once taught in Sunday School. They came from Kivulu, a slum not far from Makerere University. Every Sunday for two years I left early from my dormitory room at the university to collect the children from their impoverished dwellings and walk them to church. Every Sunday I taught them in Sunday School of their loving Father in heaven and of Jesus who had become poor that they might be rich. And every Sunday I walked them home again, feeling that I had justified myself as a religious teacher. I was not ashamed to say to these children,

"Depart in peace, be ye warm and filled." I was not ashamed to leave them in their destitute condition. To me they were only souls to save, I had no eyes to see their physical suffering.

With the faces of these children came another memory of my *own* childhood, and the poverty of my village. I was born in the deep forests of Uganda during the Great War, the first child of my father's second wife. Immediately after my birth my father moved his household to the village of Banga on the shores of Lake Victoria. There he spent long hours in his cotton and coffee fields and even longer hours picking out seeds or sorting beans to get the best price at the village market. No matter how hard he worked, there was never enough money. Other men got rich off his labor but he could not provide for his family of two wives and 10 children. The year of my twelfth birthday I had to wear five pairs of ragged shorts, all at one time, in order to look as if I was wearing one whole pair.

That same year, my mother was unable to pay my school fees. There was no free primary or secondary education in East Africa and she had saved for years to collect enough shillings for one school term. Now I was in my second term, and I could not return to school without 15 shillings. I told my mother's sister, Aunt Lusi, of my need, and she gave me her last shillings. They were tied up in a ragged knotted cloth, and as I walked away from her gate I could not help shedding tears. I wondered when God would ever change the poor conditions of my village.

I shed tears as a child for the poverty of my village because that poverty was my own. Like thousands of other children from destitute families I received my education from the hands of people who could barely feed and clothe themselves. My people had promoted

23

me to a position of honor and now, in the ivory tower of my success, I could no longer identify with their sufferings. I could teach their children and preach in their marketplaces, but I could not feel their need. My dreams of success were only for myself, I did not dream for the poor. I had become like the very people I once despised. I had become the new exploiter.

2

Stitching: Save a Child

The meeting with the fugitive family brought a revolution to my life. I was deeply touched by their poverty, and I forgot my anger at the mission administrator. I remembered instead my own responsibility before God.

One evening, after spending hours preparing a class lecture, I sat down at my desk and wrote a long letter to Mrs. Anky Rookmaaker, the wife of my art history professor at the Free University in Amsterdam. I recalled a conversation we had the past spring in which she told me of her work with destitute children in India. She had been deeply concerned for the homeless children of Uganda as well, and had offered to help begin a children's home in Kampala. At the time I was touched by her compassion, but soon forgot her proposal.

Now I wrote with a strong sense of urgency. "The situation here is explosive," I reported. "It threatens one from even making a first move. There are hundreds of children in Kampala living in miserable conditions and extreme and desperate cases are numerous. Some of these children need not only food but immediate personal care and medical attention. There is no Christian child center in Kampala to help them."

I closed with a request. "If you can help me," I said, "I would like to begin a home for these destitute children."

Mrs. Rookmaaker responded immediately, and with deep concern. She presented my request to the board members of the Dutch foundation, Stitching: Save a Child, and asked for their help. Its members had committed themselves to helping destitute children through indigenous leadership, and in only a few years they were sponsoring over 600 Indian children. Now, despite the great work already accomplished, they allowed their hearts to be touched again. In the fall of 1971, the Stitching foundation provided funds to establish a Christian children's home in Kampala.

In September of the same year, I appointed a board of trustees and together we hired a "mother" and "father." In October we found a five-bedroom house and in November the Kijomanyi Foundation Children's Home of Kampala opened its doors.[3] In only a few weeks the home was providing more than 20 destitute children with shelter, food, clothing and school fees. These were children without parents or children whose parents were unable to provide them with basic life necessities. In every case, they were children who had been rescued from the most desperate poverty.

The first to be admitted were the children of the fugitive woman. The day I drove them to their new home, I felt a healing in my heart. My resentment against the missionary disappeared and in its place was a strong sense of fulfillment. I knew then that my bitterness had grown out of impotence and insecurity—I had wanted to justify myself by holding a grudge against my brother.

This work with the orphanage brought great joy to my life but it was not a joy without tears. Each day seemed to bring with it new and unexpected problems. There was a sick cook, a leaking sink, a child without shoes. There was a child who had not written his sponsors. And always there was Bom, the orphanage messenger, knocking at our home in the middle of the night.

"Kefa, quick! Bring your car! The child Mukasa is dying!" The names changed but the message remained the same: another child from the orphanage had become sick from eating well. The road from malnutrition to good nutrition was painful and dangerous for small children. Their underdeveloped and worm-ridden digestive systems reacted violently during the period of adjustment, and a trip to the hospital was seldom avoided.

The knocking on the door of our home did not end with Bom's midnight calls. Almost every day there were new faces to greet. There were pastors reporting desperate cases from their churches and mothers holding thin, listless children in their arms. "Please take my child," they would beg. "I have no other hope. There is no one to care for us."

For every child we were able to accept, 20 were turned away. We investigated home situations and spent long hours in prayer, and in the end our decisions seemed arbitrary even to ourselves. *This child, not that one. Life for this one, a living death for that one.* The mothers of these rejected children never understood our position. *There is no room, there is another child more desperate,* these are sayings which make no sense at all to the mother of a suffering child.

At such times I regretted the letter I had sent to Mrs.

27

Rookmaaker, but these painful encounters were only the beginning of my frustrations. As founder of the home and chairman of its executive board, I had intended to give oversight from a distance, to help in organizational planning. I had not intended to spend my afternoons playing soccer. I had not intended to become mother and father, ambulance driver and plumber for 25 children. These are not the duties of a college professor, I began to say to myself. A man does not spend four years abroad studying art only to spend his nights losing sleep over another man's child. More and more I felt my work at the orphanage was an unwelcome burden.

One day in late December I went to the slums of Kivulu to collect an orphaned child, one of two children in Kivulu that I had once walked to Sunday School. Kivulu, "the mixture," was located just below the university on the lower slopes of Makerere Hill. Its streets were narrow and crowded, and I left my car on the nearest main road.

The child's home was only a 10-minute walk away but on this day I walked for more than 30 minutes. It seemed to me that Kivulu had changed since the days I had preached from its open markets and collected children for Sunday School. Its streets seemed narrower, noisier, dirtier. On almost every corner stood a crowded pub where men gathered to drink crude beer, a cheap brew made from bananas, pineapples or sorghum. The houses were small, dilapidated dwellings of iron roofs and mud walls. Only a few had concrete floors and many were unventilated except for a narrow doorway. Here and there were small enclosures for pigs and goats being sold in the market. Piles of garbage stood at the edge of the street and in every semi-private corner, human feces covered the ground.

The noise was deafening. Gramophones and radios

drummed out the latest Congolese tunes while buyers and sellers traded in the loud, crude language they called "free abuse." Butchers chopping half-spoiled meat ignored swarming flies and angrily demanded cash. Medicine men peddled good-luck charms. The young and unemployed gathered under shady backcloth trees to dance and talk. They drank beer from their clay pots and argued noisily among themselves, dreaming of jobs and money. Only the old men seemed at peace. They sat on hard benches smoking pipes and telling stories of better days, village days, which had passed.

It was teatime when I arrived at the child's home. Her guardian, Miriyamu, greeted me at the door and showed me to a wooden bench in the outer room. The dirt floor had been swept clean and the whole room tidied. In the corner was a charcoal stove and a short wooden shelf holding a few cups and plates. They were smoked and stained from age, but not dirty.

"Please wait here," Miriyamu said to me politely. "I will bring the child, Topista."

She stepped into the back room and a few minutes later returned with a small child of six or seven. Topista was dressed in her best garment and her face had been freshly oiled—possibly a bit too much—with Vaseline. She knelt down and greeted me shyly.

At just that moment the teakettle boiled. Miriyamu exclaimed and hurried to remove it from the flame. With a polite apology she excused herself, and stepped again to the back room. After a few minutes of noisy rattling she returned. In her hands was a brand new porcelain cup.

In the darkness of the front room, the porcelain cup gleamed. It gleamed on the mud walls, on the dirt floor, on the soiled garments of Miriyamu and Topista. There was nothing in the room that it did not outshine. Miriyamu wiped it carefully and placed it gently on an old rusty tray. She took other cups from the shelf and filled them all with tea. Then, with deep pleasure and good-will, Miriyamu gave the porcelain cup to me.

It was a special favor I had received many times before. It was the special favor the very poor reserved for the *abaana babowo*, the privileged class. I took the cup and sat down on the bench to drink my tea. Miriyamu rolled out a mat and sat on the floor with Topista. For a few minutes we spoke together about coffee and cotton predictions, and the tribal conflict in the north. When I finished my tea, I stood up from the bench and returned the cup to Miriyamu. She placed it gently back on the tray. She nodded to Topista and Topista too rose to leave. But first, as every good child does, she knelt before her guardian and said good-bye. Miriyamu's eyes shone with joy. "This is a most happy day," she said. "This is the day your life begins again."

As we walked out the door I remembered the bedding. To help the children in the period of transition, it was our policy at the home to have them bring their own mats and blankets. I spoke to Miriyamu but she shook her head. Topista had no mat. She had only a torn and soiled blanket. It was a blanket she placed on the dirt floor in the evening and a blanket she carefully folded up again in the morning. But it was not, Miriyamu said in humble apology, a blanket with which to start a new life.

Topista and I drove to the children's home, and on our way we laughed and joked. But in my mind I was saying, *This frivolous Miriyamu, this woman of no understanding. Why does she have a porcelain cup when Topista has no mat?* And then I thought, *No wonder the poor are poor. No wonder strangers come and collect their children.*

30

That evening I told Penina the whole story of Miriyamu and the porcelain cup. It was only my own angry thought that I kept to myself.

"Isn't that something!" Penina said when I finished my story. She smiled with pleasure. "The poor have such deep understanding!"

These were not the words I had expected to hear. *Perhaps*, I thought to myself, *Penina has not understood. She has not understood that the child Topista has no bed.*

But Penina was still speaking. "The humble poor," she said, "know a deep secret. They give from themselves, not from their surplus. They give from the abundance of their hearts."

These words from Penina caused me to look at Miriyamu with new eyes, and I was reminded of an ancient Baganda tradition. In our tribe when the table has been blessed by a rare food, like meat, each person takes a piece from his own plate and passes it to his neighbor, saying, *Okudiza guba mwoya, omuga gudiza enyanja*—"Giving flows from a good spirit as a river flows to the lake."

Giving, the proverb says, is not a matter of great possessions. It is a matter of the heart. The river gives of its waters to the lake even though the waters of the lake are many times greater.

It is this proverb that governs the giving of villagers. They offer wealthy guests their most prized possessions. They give to the city dweller in their midst their only plate. They slaughter their last goat for men who own factories or have fat salaries. And it is seldom an attempt to impress. It is only a sign of respect. It is to say, "We are humble people, but we will meet you at your level. We are humble people, but take this, it is all we have that conforms to your own high standard."

My own giving had been different. I had not come to Miriyamu's dwelling to give of my precious treasure. I had come to offer a favor, to help a poor orphaned child. "Here I am," I might have said as I stepped through the door. "Here I am, a most important person. I have come, in my spare time, to give life to the child Topista."

It was the guardian Miriyamu who had understood the proverb of *okudiza*. She was desperately poor, but she gave freely. She opened her home to an orphaned child when she could barely feed and clothe her own family. She kept a porcelain cup to give to others when she had nothing beautiful for herself. And she rejoiced for the child Topista when her own life continued without hope for change.

That night, from the words of Penina and from the humble Miriyamu, I learned a deep lesson. I learned that there is a giving to serve others and there is a giving to serve oneself. There is a giving to promote and a giving to dominate. But without love, there is only paternalism and self-importance. There is only the giving of surplus, not the giving of precious treasures.

3

Are You Being Broken?

Throughout 1971 Idi Amin's popularity in Uganda grew with rapid momentum. Except for former President Obote's most loyal supporters, there were few opponents to his regime. The educated celebrated the downfall of Obote's pompous administration and anticipated the rise of their own prestige and influence. The wealthy Asian population, Uganda's controlling commercial class, rejoiced in the preservation of their economic advantage. Even the poor, who normally gave no attention to national politics, welcomed Amin as one of their own.

It was in June of 1971 that the first of many strange rumors were heard in the streets of Kampala. Soldiers from the northern Acholi and Langi tribes claimed that hundreds of their tribesmen had been massacred by Amin's troops. In July, two Americans, a young reporter and a sociologist from Makerere University, went west to Mbarara barracks hoping to uncover a story. Both men disappeared. The rumors they had gone to investigate died away, but new rumors soon began. Doctors spoke among themselves of a colleague who had been dragged from his operating room and shot. Fishermen drinking in seaport bars whispered of bloated corpses floating along the Nile. Couriers bringing messages from outlying districts reported that hundreds of bodies lay unburied in the forests of northern Uganda.

In the optimistic climate of Amin's first year in power such stories were too distant and too bizarre to be believed. They were dismissed as lies manufactured by Obote loyalists or as exaggerated reports of sporadic violence. Everyone knew that the military occasionally resorted to severe measures to strengthen their position. Everyone knew that disruptive political and criminal forces had to be purged. No one expected a bloodless *coup.*

During this time the Christian church in Uganda basked in Amin's benevolence but faced many internal struggles. These problems had begun almost 100 years earlier, soon after the founding of the church. Christianity came to Uganda in 1877 through the dedicated efforts of Alexander Mackay, a Scottish Presbyterian missionary and trained engineer. Mackay firmly believed in the church's missionary mandate and he came to Uganda not only to save souls but to share his professional skills. The people he evangelized he also taught to make roads and build bridges, to read, to use the printing press, and to use modern methods of cultivation. His understanding of the gospel was deep, and his preaching was simple. He emphasized repentance, conversion and the ongoing confession of sins. Without ongoing confession, Mackay told the new converts, the church would lose its power and the people of God would lose their joy.

As Mackay traveled throughout Uganda winning people to Christ, he longed for the day when Ugandan Christians would cease to think of Christianity as a white man's religion. Wherever he established a new church, he emphasized the importance of local leadership. He discipled tribal chiefs and entrusted to them the responsibility for the religious instruction of their people. He used their homes as temporary mission stations. By the time he was ready to leave a village for another missionary journey, it was the tribal chief and not Alexander Mackay who had become the spiritual leader of the people.

Mackay's vision of a strong national church became a reality in his own lifetime. On October 9, 1885, the first blood of Christian martyrs was shed in Uganda. In less than a year King Mwanga, the Moslem king of Baganda, had killed more than 40 Ugandan believers. Many of those victims were Christian page boys of the Baganda court who had refused to participate in the rites of sodomy. In 1890 Mwanga was deposed and the political fortunes of the church brightened. Those who had escaped martyrdom began the task of rebuilding the church, and the next 10 years were years of unparalleled growth. With barely a handful of missionaries in the country the number of native evangelists increased steadily. By the end of the century more than 260 evangelists were preaching the gospel and 85 mission stations had been established.[4]

After the turn of the century, a new generation of missionaries arrived from England. They were men and women committed to "Commerce and Christianity," and they were unwilling to entrust the church to national leadership. As their vested economic interests began to infect evangelism programs, the national church was centralized away from the local community. The responsibility for spreading the gospel was taken from village chiefs and an ecclesiastical structure under missionary control replaced the mission stations. In only a few short years the indigenous church was cut off from its cultural roots. Imported liturgies replaced native tunes and western clothing replaced native robes. The village chief was replaced by the local pastor, and baptized Ugandans were given "Christian" or English names. With no indigenous theological convictions and often without any understanding of Christian commitment, these "converts" gave themselves by the thousands to European denominations.

For these reasons the Ugandan church never grounded itself in the life fibers of the African community. The Ugandan believer never found his cultural identity. While every Christian has a dual nationality, belonging to his human family and to the faith family, the Ugandan Christian was forced into a tripartite allegiance. He was a member of his tribe, a member of his church, and an illegitimate child of the West.

The problems created by these cultural tensions were never resolved. When Penina and I returned to Uganda in 1971 we found that the pervasiveness of western influence had alienated many Christian believers from the church. The awakening of their African conscience made it difficult for them to worship in the cultural mode of another civilization. At the same time, many national leaders were making sharp denunciations. They attacked the church as a stronghold of western religion or dismissed it as a fading remnant of Uganda's colonial past.

The one indigenous group which might have provided spiritual leadership during this time was the East African Revival Fellowship. The Revival Fellowship began in the 1930s when several Christian believers began meeting together for prayer.

They soon discovered that though they were busy having Bible studies, holding prayer meetings and attending church services, the things they were doing were not the central message of Christ's teaching. They had to ask themselves, did Jesus die for our meetings? Or was it for something else?

They found that Jesus had given the instruction that, before they enjoyed their devotional life, they were to be reconciled with their brother or sister whom they might have wronged during the day.[5] It was not for their devotions Christ died. What He had paid the price for was their relationship with God and one another.

I walked into my first Revival Fellowship meeting shortly after my conversion in 1961. It was Friday afternoon and the hall was packed with people singing and praising God. Most of the songs were about the blood of the Lamb that was slain. As different brethren stood up and openly confessed their sin, I noticed that no one was paying any attention to the sins confessed. Before a brother or sister could finish the confession, the rest of the brethren burst out into songs of praise.

Even though my legs were trembling, I finally stood up as well. I confessed my past unfaithfulness to God and the damaged relationships in my life. Before I had finished people started singing praises for the blood of the Lamb. I resumed my seat and one brother came and embraced me. I could feel the warmth in his hand as he said, "This is victory, brother!"

Is this the fellowship? I asked myself. *These brothers hardly noticed my sin.*

Later one of the founding fathers, Mondo, explained to me, "What we hear is not your sin, but God's work in your life. We hear you giving witness to God's power to break the chains of sin. Because we know that, left to ourselves, we can never go to a brother and confess to him, 'I have done foolishly, forgive me.' This only happens when grace takes over and pushes our pride into a tight corner."

Mondo went on to explain the power of the Spirit that is unleashed by repentance. When there is repentance, pride gives way and in its place is conviction and confession, and then forgiveness.

"Remember James 5:16," he said. " 'Confess your faults one to another, and pray one for another, that ye may be healed.' It is not the man who has the correct exegesis of this verse who knows its truth. It is the man who confesses his sin to his neighbor."

Every time I met Mondo he would greet me with the threefold challenge:

"Are you repenting?

"Are you walking in the light?

"Are you being broken?"

His questions were intended to challenge the kind of fellowship I was having with the Christians with whom I was doing mission work. He suspected that we were using our concern for our mission project to avoid the real work of God in our lives.

It was Mondo who taught me that walking in the light means a total sharing with my brother of my secrets. He reminded me of Christ's words to His disciples, "I no longer call you servants, a servant knows not the secrets of his lord but I have shared with you the secrets of my father."[6]

"When we share our secrets," Mondo said, "there is a total identification with our brother. We have a reciprocal bond. There is no room left for gossip. Nothing needs to be talked over in secret which is already in the light. Gossip is converted into efforts to seek solutions together. Instead of majoring on a brother's weakness, we can defend him where he is weak and promote him where he is strong.

"We must become *okumenyeka*. We must be 'broken,' even as Jesus was broken for the world. To be broken is to have no pride, for where there is pride there is no confession and no forgiveness. The broken one is he who is broken to heal a broken relationship. He is the one willing to 'give in,' who doesn't find his identity in always being in the right."

One day a brother of the Revival Fellowship came to me and read from his Bible:

> *And taking the five loaves and the two fish he looked up to heaven, and blessed, and broke and gave the loaves to the disciples, and the disciples gave them to the crowds.* [7]

The brother looked at me sternly, "Until God breaks your will," he said, "He will never use you. You will remain only a nice loaf of bread." He explained to me that unless I was broken I would be too proud to lose my life for sinners. I would be too proud to give my life away for people who were not perfect. I would wait for the perfect person and the perfect community, and I would never find them. I would end up like Judas, making only a partial commitment to the body of believers to whom I belonged and finding my identity in my rebellion from them.

The brother challenged me to follow the example of Jesus who while we were yet sinners allowed His body to be broken. "Our commitment to one another in community can be no less than His," he said. "We must say to one another, this is my body broken for you. I am laying all my professional skills, abilities and economic

39

resources at your disposal. Take them and use them as you see fit."

Gradually I came to understand what Mondo was saying. If I was having a Bible study and disowning my brother, I was not repenting. If I was going to church and keeping my brother at a distance I was not walking in the light. Without a willingness to live a transparent, broken life before my brethren, our meetings were just another form of alienation. They were religious counterfeits.

Now, it was 1971 and 10 years had passed since I had learned these truths from Mondo. Most of the original leaders of the Revival Fellowship were dead. The Revival Fellowship was no longer broken by repentance, but by dissension. Its members had separated into two groups, the awakened and the non-awakened. The awakened were extremely legalistic, the non-awakened were socially more progressive. Both groups were so bitterly opposed to each other that their abusive attitudes were eventually reported by the national newspaper.

One day in September when my own heart was heavy with the church's struggles, I was visited in my home by Katongole Sabaganzi. Katongole was a distinguished man with a bald head and royal features. He had been a private advisor to the last Baganda king and he was well known as an outspoken critic of the westernization of Ugandan culture. On this day Katongole wore the long white traditional robe of Baganda men and we talked together for several hours about the present crises of the Ugandan church. The longer we talked, the more angry Katongole became. Finally, he could contain himself no longer. He stood up from his chair and, glaring with wisdom, delivered an impassioned lecture.

"The church has made many mistakes," Katongole

said, pronouncing each word distinctly. "We have had political independence for 10 years and the church is not yet free. But if after all these years of hearing the gospel we are still criticizing those who brought the message, that is the biggest mistake of all. It is not the fault of the signpost if the wayfarer sits beneath it. It is not the fault of the westerner if Ugandans do not take their church where it needs to go. It is time for us to take responsibility for our own house."

Katongole took a deep breath and continued speaking. "We are like Samuel and Eli in the Bible," he said. "For all of Samuel's life he worked in the Temple and all his life, Eli stood between him and God. Then when Samuel came of age God called him. But Samuel went to Eli. He knew that it was Eli who was the professional servant of God. He knew that Eli was the man with the vision. Samuel could not believe that God wanted to talk to him alone.

"This is how we Christians in Uganda act. God has called us to Himself, but our eyes have been turned to the West. Instead of hearing God's message to us as Africans, we have heard an enculturated gospel. We cannot believe that God wants to speak to us in our own language. We cannot believe that He wants to speak to us alone!"

Katongole's words were most inspiring. I had thought often of the cultural tensions in the Ugandan church. Now, it seemed, the time for thinking had come to an end. Katongole had said it, it was not a time for sitting. It was a time to act.

That evening, with the thoughts Katongole and I shared together still fresh in my mind, I sat down at my desk and wrote a long essay. Not long afterwards, the essay was published in pamphlet form by the University of Makerere Press. The pamphlet circulated extensively among the educated, and many men and women began joining our student Bible study. Out of the study grew a prayer group which was attended not only by students but by professors, nurses, preachers, businessmen and office workers. We came together once a week at the home of my friend Adoniya Kirinda and as we prayed and sang together, we asked God to bring salvation to His people. We were all from different missionary camps, some were Anglicans, some were Baptists, some Pentecostals, some Roman Catholics. Despite our differences we had this in common: we had all experienced a new birth in Christ and we had a burning zeal for evangelism. We wanted to reach out to our community with the good news of the gospel. We wanted to tell our fellow Ugandans that they did not have to forsake their cultural selves to become Christians. They did not have to forsake their villages, their clans, their music. God was going to speak to them as Africans.

We made plans to convert the city of Kampala, but we found that it was we ourselves who needed conversion. Before we could be lights in our community, we needed to be lights to one another. Most of us had in various ways tried to be evangelists in our own rights. In the mission command we had heard as young converts, the emphasis had been on *go*, not *love*. It was the ministry, not the brethren, that was most important. As a result we had come to love our sermons more than the people to whom we preached. We had come to love the faceless converts of mass evangelism more than our brothers and sisters in Christ.

Now as the Holy Spirit began to unite our hearts we saw that before the Great Commission, came the commandment: love one another. We were to confess and reject our disagreements. In the past we had majored on our differences—Anglicans did not say hello to Baptists and, when a Pentecostal met a Roman Catholic, he did not feel that he was meeting a brother. But now we heard God's call to live broken lives before one another. We were not to build our fellowship on the foundation of baptism, tongues or liturgy. We were to build on the reconciling blood of Jesus Christ.

The first stage of our evangelistic fervor ended in the humbling experience of daily confession. We confessed to one another our personal jealousies and competitive strivings. We confessed the sinful resentments in our hearts. We learned that a broken relationship is a poison and the Bible made no exceptions: both the offended and the offender were equally guilty before God. We were to seek out those we thought might have something against us. If someone wronged us, we had the obligation to rebuke him. If he repented, we had the obligation to forgive him.

One evening, at the end of a long prayer meeting, an elderly evangelist from the Revival Fellowship came to speak with me. He was a tall, thin man from the western Banyankole tribe, and he had been an evangelist for many years. "Kefa," he said, speaking in a most sober manner, "I have something to tell you. I have been listening to you pray and your prayers are not as they should be. You pray to indulge your own desires. You center on your needs or the needs of the brethren, but you do not center on Christ."

I was offended by these strong words from the evangelist and I tried to explain to him the motivation for my prayers. "Christ is the center of our needs," I said; "God has commanded us to bring all our burdens to Him."

The evangelist only shook his head. "Christ is the center of our needs," he said, "but He is first the center of our lives. Before we pray concerning our desires, we must understand God's desires and let them shape our own. Otherwise when we pray we are only reinforcing our own self-centeredness."

The message that this brother brought was a hard one to hear but as I began to understand its meaning, I joined with my brothers and sisters in a new discipline of prayer. Together we determined to make Christ the beginning and the end of all our expectations. We determined to have no hope except that which was derived from Scripture. We learned that prayer was not a platform for self-expression but a self-emptying process.

As we humbled ourselves before God and sought to make His desires our own, the bond of love which grew between us spread outward to our families and to our friends. We learned to share the gospel within the context of our occupations and our culture. We began to understand that evangelism was not a program or a method, but a life-style of submission and service to others. More and more people joined our fellowship. By the end of 1971, our Bible studies and all-night prayer group had grown too large to be accommodated in a single house. We moved to a local YMCA and began meeting on Sunday afternoons for worship services. I shared preaching responsibilities with a minister from Ghana, and through the evangelizing efforts of a core of zealous young men, the number attending our Sunday services increased remarkably. By May of 1972 we were forced to meet outdoors on the extensive grounds belonging to a wealthy member of our congregation. By June we were over 4,000 strong and a council of 35 elders directed the affairs of our new church, the Redeemed Church of Uganda.

This sudden growth gave us a deep sense of expectancy and optimism for the future. We looked forward to the day when revival would come to Kampala. Only once our hearts were sobered. At the close of a special

44

Friday meeting, when we had spent the entire night in personal confession of sin, a brother from the Revival Fellowship stood up and spoke this warning:

"Brothers and sisters, I fear there is too much brokenness here. We are walking too much in the light. We must remember that the devil will not stand for this."

He was silent for a moment. Then he trembled, and he spoke these words, "It is a frightening thing to be a child of God."

4
Take Us Too!

On August 4, 1972, General Amin stood before soldiers stationed on Uganda's eastern border and announced the expulsion of Uganda's Asian population. He explained that God had spoken to him in a dream, directing him to act immediately and "win the economic war." The Asians, an affluent middle-class community of merchants and technicians, had 90 days to leave the country.

Two days after this astonishing announcement, I went with an elder from the church to visit with the Martin Okelo family. Martin Okelo was a distinguished Ugandan from the Langi tribe and a former member of the national parliament. On the previous Sunday he and his family had attended our worship service for the first time. After the service Okelo came with his wife and

two sons to make introductions. He spoke of his deep
interest in the message of Jesus Christ and asked me to
his home for a longer discussion with other members of
the family.

The Okelos lived in a large white stucco mansion on
Nakasero Hill and we arrived at their home in the late
afternoon as the sun was just setting over the valley. A
blossoming flame tree stood at their front gate and a wall
of hibiscus shrubs enclosed the well-kept flower gardens
of their enormous yard. The entire atmosphere was one
of aristocratic affluence. As we walked to the front door
I began to wonder if I was dressed properly and I tried
to think how I would begin my message.

The door was half open. We knocked and stepped
inside. Beneath our feet was a beautiful light green carpet. A zebra skin hung in the hallway and through the
door of the sitting room I could see colorful batiks and
expensive European furniture.

We waited for our host for several minutes. No one
came to welcome us. When we called out a greeting,
there was only silence. I began to think we had come to
the wrong house and I turned to my friend to suggest
that we leave. Just at that moment a small boy appeared
in the doorway of the sitting room. He stood completely
still and his arms were raised straight in the air.

Even in the half-light of the hallway I recognized the
child as Okelo's youngest son. I moved towards him,
strangely moved by his haunting appearance and deeply
puzzled. He began to cry and tried to speak but his
words were lost in sobs. Before I could reach him he fell
completely stiff to the floor.

I bent down to pick up the child. As I did, I looked
beyond him into the sitting room. A deep shock passed
through my body. The curtains were open and the sun
was shining through onto a carpet covered with blood

and excrement. Broken teeth and eyes pulled from their sockets were scattered throughout the room. On a table in the center of the floor three human tongues were laid out in a row, as if on public display.

Without thinking I grabbed young Okelo from the floor and with the elder I ran shaking and trembling from the house. The short distance to our parking space seemed to be many miles and with every sound I thought myself a dead man. Finally we reached the car, and I laid the boy on the back seat. The elder and I took our own seats in deep fear and I drove quickly towards my home. Throughout the trip the boy remained motionless, his arms raised rigidly over his head.

When we arrived at the house I put Okelo on a couch and stared helplessly at his paralyzed body. His hands were cold and his eyes stared straight ahead, seeing nothing. Later I learned that he was the sole survivor from a nightmare of death. Soldiers from the army of Idi Amin had come to his home late in the evening. They had raped his mother and tortured to death each member of his family. Twelve-year-old Okelo was somehow overlooked. When the killing was over and the soldiers had left, he crawled under his bed. He had stayed there for more than a day, his mind empty and his body paralyzed. It wasn't until he heard our voices in the hallway that he had been able to move.

Now, once again, the boy's body was stiff, his mind completely closed to human contact. I tried to comfort him but no words or gestures could reach him. There was no sign of life in his eyes. In utter frustration I picked up my Bible and began to read out loud. I read chapter after chapter. I read of the Christ who promised to see His children beyond the grave. I read of the Redeemer who claimed that the words of His mouth were life and spirit. My own words failed me. I could make no interpretations. I had nothing to say to the small shattered life lying before me. I did not think that the truths I meditated on every morning could reach his deaf ears.

When I looked up from my reading, Okelo was lowering his arms. His neck was no longer stiff and he turned his head to look at my face. There were tears in his eyes but beyond his tears there was life and hope. He looked away again, breathed deeply and closed his eyes.

I took Okelo's hand in mine and prayed to God, thanking Him for His providential care. I confessed my own astonishment. I knew it was in spite of my unbelief that the child responded; it was in spite of my skepticism that God's Spirit had come among us. Now I wanted to cry out, like Peter, "Depart from me; for I am a sinful man, O Lord."[8]

The healing of Okelo was complete. Later that night I drove him to the Kijomanyi Children's Home and he was admitted to the home as a ward of the foundation. When I saw him again the following day he was playing soccer in the yard, running and shouting with the other children. He made many friends and before long he adjusted to the poorer, communal circumstances of his new life.

Okelo was the first of many children to come to the Kijomanyi Home as a result of brutal killings by Amin's soldiers. In the months that followed the murder of the Okelo family, Amin orphaned thousands of Ugandan children. Soon in every town and village there were dozens of young boys and girls who had witnessed the torturous, bestial deaths of their parents. As I traveled throughout southern Uganda collecting children for the home, I heard many terrifying stories. And I became convinced that the regime of Idi Amin was not merely tyrannical but demonic.

One day, late in 1972, I drove to a large village six miles outside of Kampala to collect a child by the name of Florence. Florence was almost 10 years old and her parents had been dead for several years. Now she lived with her guardians on the slope of a hill in a small, poorly thatched mud hut. By the side of the hut was a tiny garden of corn and sweet potatoes, but the soil was bad and the crops had withered. The family did not own a stove and a few rocks piled in the yard supported their only cooking pot.

Florence and her guardian stood outside the hut and greeted me politely. The child was wearing only a small, dirty cloth wrapper. The guardian was dressed in a skirt so soiled and stained that its original color could not be determined. We spoke together for several moments. During this time a small crowd of well-dressed children gathered around us. I was surprised to see them in such poor surroundings. The guardian explained to me that they were children from prominent families whose parents had been killed by the soldiers of Idi Amin.

As she spoke, a small boy stepped forward to confirm her words. He told how he and his brothers and sisters watched their parents die. "The soldiers came in the middle of the night," he said. "They made everyone get out of bed. They pushed us into the living room. Then they grabbed my father and cut him open with their bayonets. They give his insides to my mother and laughed at her when she wouldn't eat them. So they kicked her and they choked her and she died."

The boy told his story without emotion, in the articulate manner of children raised in educated homes. I could not comprehend the situation he described, but I was moved to tears. I wondered what would become of him and the entire bruised generation of children which was to be Uganda's future.

I said good-bye to the guardian and walked away. Florence followed me. When I turned to lift her onto the front seat of the car, the other children crowded in around her. I had to pull them out one by one and as I did, each one pleaded with me in desperation: "Take us! Take us too!"

I tried to explain to them that there was not enough room in the home, that each child had to be chosen by a committee, but they only stared at me with empty faces. I could see that they thought I was lying. They were convinced that I could take them all if only I had wanted to do it.

As I took my seat, I promised to remember them, but these words sounded hollow even to myself. When I drove away the children chased my car and I could see them in my mirror, running in the dust. Finally, one by one, they gave up, exhausted.

It was then that I felt the deep pain which had been growing in my heart. *Oh Lord,* I cried silently, *where is your concern for these children? Why am I taking one when there are 10 others? Why can't you give me the chance to save them all?*

Feeling desperate and abused, I looked over at Florence. She straightened her cloth wrapper. Since her parents' death she had known nothing but hardship. Her poverty-stricken guardians had used her as a slave laborer and she had never had enough to eat. Now her face beamed in anticipation.

I stared at Florence and in the deep silence of my frustration I heard the convicting voice of Jesus: "Kefa, you are not the Messiah. You are not in charge of my vineyard. You are only one small worker, and this is the task that I have for you. This is the child I want you to take."

In this humbling service of collecting orphaned children, God taught me of my own expendability. The need was far greater than all my resources and my limitations in light of the enormity of evil haunted me. I felt useless in God's Kingdom. But in this brokenness I learned that it was not I who was sufficient but God. It was He who had provided the vision and it was He who would provide the ability. From the beginning to the end it was His work.

5

Jolly Joe Is Here!

In September of 1972 a small band of Ugandan exiles attempted to overthrow the government of Idi Amin. They were mostly soldiers from the Acholi and Langi tribes who had fled Uganda with Obote in 1971 and they came over the border with less than 15 hundred men. As they moved north towards Kampala they were decisively defeated in a three-hour battle at Mbarara barracks. The following day, over Radio Uganda, Amin announced his army's successful defense against "the September Invasion." The fighting had been fierce, he claimed, but troops from Tanzania, Great Britain and Israel had been overcome and driven beyond Uganda's border.

The September Invasion provided Amin with the excuse he needed for a new wave of killings. On September 21, armed soldiers broke into the chamber of the chief justice of Uganda and, after humiliating him in front of the court, dragged him away at gunpoint. He was taken to Makindye Military Prison where his ears, nose, lips and private parts were cut from his body. After two hours of suffering, he was disemboweled and the rest of his body was burned.

One week after the death of the chief justice an unexpected visitor attended the morning service of the Redeemed Church. I had just finished preaching when a friend approached me with the news. "Joseph Kiwanuka is here," he said in an excited whisper. "He wants to see you!" And before I could respond he had grabbed my arm and was leading me through the crowd to where Kiwanuka stood.

Joseph "Jolly Joe" Kiwanuka was one of Uganda's wealthiest and most influential citizens, and a stubborn, strong-willed man. He owned a large wholesale business in Kampala and was the owner and director of Uganda's champion soccer team, Express. He drove through the streets of Kampala in an expensive, red, American-made car and his unpredictable behavior and complete disregard for public opinion had made him a legend even to his closest friends. They had nicknamed him *Namawatulira*, "I will tell him," because he was a man who knew no middle language. If he thought someone to be a fool he told him so and in the most frank vocabulary. On more than one occasion, while watching his team compete, he had rushed onto the soccer field, stopped the game and, with a barrage of verbal abuse, forced the referee to reverse his decision.

In the same straightforward manner, Kiwanuka had made his views on religion notorious throughout Uganda. He was an atheist and a humanist and he considered religion, tribal and western, to be an inhuman political tool by which the powerful suppressed the helpless and robbed them of their freedom. Once during a close match between his own soccer team and a Catholic school he had slapped a priest from the opposing team across the face. Later, when reporters asked him why he struck the man, Kiwanuka refused to answer. He only said, "There is no God," and walked away.

Now as I caught sight of Kiwanuka standing by himself at the edge of the compound I was apprehensive. He was a huge man, well over six feet tall and heavy. He parted his hair down the middle, a fashion which he had introduced in Kampala (and which former President Obote himself had imitated), and his entire appearance was one of distinction and arrogance.

I greeted him formally but he did not even bother to shake hands.

"*Owanga*," he said abruptly, speaking in the language of our tribe, the Baganda, "You know what's going on. What do you say about it?"

I knew that he was speaking of the growing brutality of Amin and his soldiers but before I could answer, he spoke again.

"How do you see it?" he said in the same intense manner. "Do you think God knows what's going on? Do you think He is going to help us?"

This is not Jolly Joe Kiwanuka, I thought to myself, strangely moved. This man is desperate and defeated. But my suspicions of him as an atheist and a blasphemer ran deep and I answered him in the most guarded words of our language. "If He so wishes," I replied.

Kiwanuka was silent. He stared at me for a moment and then walked away, a remote and solitary figure. I wanted to run after him and say something of substance but no words came to mind. When he disappeared in the crowd I turned back to greet other visitors and members from the congregation.

In the following week I thought many times of Kiwanuka. I remembered the short conversation we had together and I wondered why he had come to church. The Kiwanuka I saw that Sunday morning bore no resemblance at all to the arrogant and self-assured speaker I had seen and heard on dozens of television and radio shows. What happened to change Kampala's leading citizen into such a desperate and haunted man?

The first time I ever heard Kiwanuka speak publicly was during my first year in England as a student at the Royal College of Art. It was November of 1969 and Kiwanuka had come to London to bury Mutesa II, the last Baganda king. The Baganda, the southern tribe of Uganda to which both Kiwanuka and I belonged, were traditional enemies of President Milton Obote's tribe, the northern Langi. King Mutesa had been Obote's most outspoken and bitter opponent and in 1966, after an attack on his palace in which many Baganda were killed, he was forced to flee to England. He spent his last years living in London, where he died in early winter of 1969.

King Mutesa's memorial service, which I attended, was full of spies from Obote's extensive international network. The presence of these informers forced the speakers to choose their words carefully and, one by one, they made a point of disassociating themselves from the king's politics. It was in this atmosphere of tension and diplomacy that Joseph "Jolly Joe" Kiwanuka stood up to speak. As the founder of the Ugandan National Congress and a member of parliament, he commanded immediate respect. Dressed in a gray, tailored suit he looked once around the room with a cool and confident gaze. Then, in a loud voice, he addressed himself to Obote's agents.

"You spies," he said scornfully, "I know you are here. It is nothing to me. If there is something I say that you want Obote to hear, you come tell me first. I'll take you to the airport and pay for your plane ticket home."

The audience was completely silent. Kiwanuka stared sternly at each person he suspected of spying and then he continued.

"You spies are here," he said, now speaking almost quietly, "because we black people have not learned to love ourselves. I have been all over the world. I have been to America, to Australia, to Europe and to Asia. Everywhere, black people live in the most miserable conditions. We live in the sewers of society. I tell you, we are alone. There is no man who cares for us. We will not be loved unless we learn to love ourselves."

Kiwanuka continued his remarks with praise for King Mutesa and then sat down. Only a few persons came forward to shake his hand and he left the meeting alone. Several weeks later the news reached London from Uganda that Joseph Kiwanuka had been arrested and imprisoned without a trial.

When I saw Kiwanuka again it was in March of 1971, in a newsreel shown in Holland not long after Amin's takeover. The film was taken at Luzira prison on the day Amin released Obote's prisoners. The streets were lined with thousands of people gathered to celebrate the liberation and the first man to step outside the prison gate was Joseph Kiwanuka. He raised his arm in a jubilant salute and the crowd greeted him with a great shout.

I heard nothing more of Kiwanuka until the day he came to the Redeemed Church. When I stood up to preach on the Sunday following his visit, I looked over the congregation hoping to see him, but he was not there.

It was early in November before he came to church a second time. Then, after the service we spoke again. In the same serious manner, Kiwanuka repeated his questions. "How do you see things? Is there a God? Does He know what is going on?"

"God is there," I said, forgetting my fears and suspicions. "Have you considered that we ought to give ourselves entirely over to Him?"

"I have considered it," Kiwanuka said in an urgent voice. "What is to be done?"

We walked together to a small house by the side of the compound and there we prayed, asking God to reveal Himself. When we finished, Kiwanuka was weeping. I knew then that some desperate tension had overtaken his life, and the depths of his anguish caused my own heart to mourn. Later I learned that he had been an unwilling witness to the torturous death of the chief justice of Uganda, a man whom he had loved deeply. In that moment, when Kiwanuka had stood over the mutilated remains of his friend, the foundations of his life had been destroyed. The chief justice and he had worked together for more than 20 years, sacrificing themselves to make Uganda a strong, free country. Now it seemed that both of their lives had come to nothing.

When Kiwanuka finished weeping, he was silent for a moment. Then he turned to me with a grave but more settled face and said, "So there really is a Kingdom."

They were strange words and I did not fully understand them. But I did understand that new life had come to Kiwanuka and, as we embraced, the power of God in his life brought new strength and courage to my own.

Two weeks later at the end of our Sunday worship service, Joseph Kiwanuka stood before the congregation of the Redeemed Church and spoke of the grace of God.

"From the beginning," he said, speaking in a strong and powerful voice, "I have been looking for a kingdom. I have been looking for a kingdom of freedom. I believed in the goodness of man and I believed that men and women could learn to love each other. Now I tell you, there is no good man. If God will leave us in our natural state, we will eat grass as the goats."

Kiwanuka continued, and his voice rang throughout the compound. "But God has not left us!" he exclaimed. "He has made for us the Kingdom that we cannot make for ourselves. He has rescued us from our own corruption and cruelty. The chains of our evil have been broken. It is I, Joseph Kiwanuka, who am speaking and I know what I am saying! I have met the man of freedom, Jesus Christ. My sins have been forgiven. I stand before you as a new member of God's Kingdom."

Kiwanuka's public confession of Jesus Christ was most astonishing. Within days after the service, the entire city of Kampala was humming with the news. "Have you heard? Jolly Joe has become an Aleluya man!" The story was told with skepticism and laughter. Kiwanuka had been too notorious, his views on religion too outspoken, for people to believe easily in his conversion. Even within the church itself, members remained cynical. More than once, I was warned to be careful. Kiwanuka, it was said, was using his identification with the church to further his own political aspirations.

Kiwanuka was aware of his critics, but he ignored them. He continued to speak boldly of his new life in Christ, and hundreds of people from all over Uganda began coming to the Redeemed Church on Sunday morning just to see him sitting in church. Kiwanuka frequently spoke to the congregation before the service and more than once he prefaced his remarks with a half-joking reference to his status as Uganda's most brilliant and notorious citizen.

"Listen," he once said, speaking from the center of the church compound, "it is I, Joseph Kiwanuka, who is speaking, and I am one of the wisest men. If you count the three wisest men in this country and do not count me, you do not know how to count!"

Privately, Kiwanuka was a man of deep devotion. He spent many hours fasting and praying, and from the beginning he was a serious student of the Bible. His maturity and commitment were soon apparent to me, and in January of 1973 I appointed him chairman of the church board. Even then, there were many people who remained unconvinced of his sincerity. It was only months later, in the midst of great suffering and sadness, that we all saw most clearly what God had done in the life of Joseph Kiwanuka.

6

Thunder in the Fire

It was a cool Sunday afternoon in November, not long after Kiwanuka's conversion. I was walking from the vestry to the pulpit to begin the morning service when I heard someone calling me, *"Sebo, Sebo!* Reverend, Reverend!" The voice was excited and determined, and as I turned towards the sound I saw a small, thin woman pushing her way through the crowd. With one hand she waved at me wildly and with the other she held the arm of a young boy. Both their faces were glowing with excitement. Behind them, following closely, was a short, stout woman with a sullen, heavy face.

"Sebo!" The cheerful-faced woman was breathing heavily as she blocked my path to the pulpit. "I have a great matter to tell you, Sebo."

And I have a sermon to preach, I thought. But the

woman rushed on without allowing me to speak.

"Here is my son!" she said, pushing the young boy forward and making a polite introduction. "He is the one you healed. We came to your meeting two weeks ago and his leg was completely stiff. He had never even walked. Now look!" She pointed to the boy's leg. "He can run!"

The boy looked at me shyly, but his face was beaming. He was a small child, not more than 12 years of age, and he was dressed in a white shirt and khaki shorts. He demonstrated the words of his mother by bending his leg back and forth, and jumping about. When he finished with these simple exercises, he came and stood by my side. He smiled up at me, as if perhaps I was his own father, and I found myself feeling uncomfortable.

"I am sorry," I said, speaking to the mother and glancing towards the pulpit. "There has been a misunderstanding. I have never seen you and your son before."

"No," the woman said, shaking her head decisively. "There is no misunderstanding. My son and I heard your announcement. You are the one who healed him!"

I could only stare. The claim the woman made seemed preposterous to me and I was puzzled by her persistence. What could she want? Why should she tell this strange story in such a public place? The woman sensed my skepticism and, with her son nodding his head vigorously in support of her claims, she began a lengthy explanation.

"Two weeks ago, my son and I went for a weekly consultation with our witch doctor." The mother turned and pointed to the stout woman now standing beside her. "This woman attempted many cures and even passed the boy through the fire, but his leg was still lame. That's how it has been since he was a baby. When we left the witch I thought to myself that the boy would never get better, and I was very tired. We have been making these consultations for years. They are so expensive and my husband is not one who has money.

"We took a short cut from the usual way to the bus stop and the boy was limping. That's when we saw all the people and heard their singing. We crossed the street to see if it was a festival but just as we arrived all the singing stopped and everyone was quiet. We heard your voice speaking a blessing, and the people saying 'Amen,' and that's when I knew it was a church. I turned to leave, but the boy grabbed my arm and started jumping up and down and shouting. When I looked down at his leg he was bending it back and forth. We were both so excited! Then there was a great commotion all around us. We've tried to find you ever since to tell you of this wonder, but the crowd has always been too big!"

The woman ended her story and I was so astonished that I forgot my rush to the pulpit. I tried to explain to her, even as I kept an eye on her witch doctor companion, that I had no magic power. If her son had been healed while I pronounced the benediction, it was not I who had healed him, but Jesus Christ.

"What you have seen," I said, "is the power of the living Lord!"

It was just then that the witch doctor spoke for the first time. "That's what I want," she said in a low but aggressive voice. "I want this power. Will you give it to me?" And before I even understood her question, she knelt down on the ground in front of my feet.

The people around us turned to stare. I realized that soon there would be another commotion, but I did not feel so much embarrassed as afraid. First there had been a strange healing, and now here was a witch doctor who wanted power. I wondered who she was and where she had come from. *Isn't this a woman who has power over evil spirits?* I asked myself. *Isn't this a woman who can sit in fire?* My western education had taught me to question the existence of demons and the powers of their servants, but I never forgot a strange experience I had as a child in the home of a shrine priestess.

In August of 1953, at the age of 12, I left my home village of Banga and came to live in the village of Nantule, 30 miles away, where I was to be a student in Kiyoola Primary School. From the beginning, my mother had been determined to send me to school. When I was still young she taught me a chorus which she had learned from a passing traveler:

> When you wake up in the morning
> Before doing any work
> First read in the Book
> Jesus caused to be written.
> You kneel before Him.
> In the presence of the living God
> He will bless you
> As you tell Him everything.

We would sing this song together and my mother, who could neither read nor write, would speak of her secret ambition.

"Kefa," she would say sternly, "when you are grown, you will go to school. You will learn to read and we will know about this Book whose author is Jesus."

When I was eight an evangelist came to Banga. I immediately attached myself to him and every morning I rose early to help him build his thatched-roof church. In the evening he came to our home and while my mother listened in great excitement, he taught me to say the alphabet and to read simple words. But before long termites invaded the church we had built together, and the whole structure tumbled down. The evangelist left our village and never returned.

His departure left my mother disappointed, but she would not be defeated. She began saving shillings to pay for my school fees. Because my father was a poor cotton and coffee farmer who had money in his home for only a few weeks at a time, it was four years before she was able to collect enough shillings for one school term. It was then, at the age of 12, that I said good-bye to Banga and to my childhood.

My mother took me to Nantule herself, and we traveled on foot. It was my first time away from home. As we walked on small winding paths through heavy trees and tangled climbing plants my mother explained to me about the gods. The god of the forest was not the same as the god of the grasslands; the god of the grasslands was not the same as the god of the lake. There were many other gods as well. There were gods of planting, of harvesting, of prosperity. There were gods of the earth and gods of the heaven. When I was older I would learn their names. For now it was enough that I learn to serve the living God; I was going to Nantule to learn about Jesus.

We came to a river and, where the water narrowed, we crossed over a small wooden bridge. I stared curiously at someone bathing below.

"Be careful," my mother warned, pushing me along. "It might be *Omusambwa.* She is the river goddess and she will strike you blind!"

For the rest of our journey I was quiet in fear. I had not known the world was so full of gods.

When we arrived in Nantule my mother placed me in the hands of a guardian family and left me with this stern warning: "Son, until you are able to read do not come back to me."

As she walked away, I began to cry. She did not stop or turn her head, and it was then that I knew she too was shedding tears.

The home my mother left me in was the home of a shrine priestess and only a few hours after my arrival I was taken to the shrine to meet my hostess and pay respect to the gods, "the elders" of the home. The shrine was a round, thatched-roof hut in back of the main house. It was surrounded by an elephant grass fence and as I walked towards it I could hear singing and the sounds of rattling gourds and beating drums. Behind the shrine was a small grove of shrunken coffee trees and their bare, neglected branches made me wish I was home again in Banga.

"*Ingira, tukulamusiza!* Come in, my child. We welcome you to our home!"

A deep male voice greeted me from the interior of the shrine as I peered nervously through its doorway. I stood hesitating on the threshold until I heard the command repeated and then, taking a deep breath, I stepped inside. For a moment I was surrounded by darkness. When my eyes grew accustomed to the dim half-light of the room, I found myself standing among a small group of people who were sitting on a floor of lemon grass. They stared at me curiously as I looked nervously around the room.

In the center of the shrine were four roof poles embroidered with colored reeds and backcloths, and through the poles I saw a log hearth covered with goatskins. The hearth was protected by a barrier of raised spears and shields, and behind the barrier was a burning fire. In the hot coals of the fire sat a woman!

I stared at her in astonishment, and she welcomed me in the same deep male voice I had heard from the doorway. "Come here, my child. Do not be afraid. I am glad to see you and you will soon be happy in your new home."

My heart was beating furiously as I knelt and returned her greeting in the manner my mother had taught me. The woman smiled at me, pleased at my politeness, but my own face was frozen in fear. Who was this woman who could sit in the middle of a scorching hot fire and not be burned? Why did she speak like a man? I stared at the flames licking around her clothes but I could see nothing unusual in her dress. She wore a simple cloth garment, like the women of my own village, and her hair was well-trimmed. There were no tribal scars on her face. Her one exceptional feature was her kindness to me, a small child and a stranger in her home.

The woman was my hostess, and when she had finished her greeting she told me of the chores I was expected to perform in my new home.

"While you are a guest here," she said, still speaking in a male voice, "it is your duty to tend the fires of the shrine."

Looking back, I do not know why I answered the shrine priestess as I did. I knew nothing about Jesus except the chorus my mother had taught me, but somehow I felt that I was already in His service and that it would be wrong to serve in the shrine of another god.

"I cannot tend your fires," I said, hoping not to offend the priestess. "My mother has sent me here to learn to read the Book."

The words were barely out of my mouth when my hostess was overcome with a shaking rage. She thundered, and the devotees sitting closest to her covered their heads. I stared at the convulsed woman in terror. Seconds later a young girl grabbed my arm and pulled me away from the hearth.

"That is not my mother's voice speaking to you," she

said, whispering in fear. "It is the god of thunder. You must do whatever he tells you!"

Just then the god repeated his command and my legs trembled. I had never spoken with a god before and I did not understand why he would be so angry. But I was more certain than ever that I could not tend the fires of his shrine. My mother had sent me to Nantule to learn to read about Jesus.

Almost against my will, I refused a second time. The god thundered again and when he spoke the deep male voice was no longer kind. "If you continue in your stubbornness," he said, "you will die in the first drizzling rain. Lightning will strike you dead."

With this promise, the thundering came to an end. The woman moved from the fire and sat down near the hearth on a leopard skin. She spread a black goatskin in front of her feet and with both hands picked up an ivory horn filled with cowrie shells and coffee beans. She was ready to begin her divination, but first, without looking up, she ordered me from the shrine.

My first night in my new home I spent lying on the floor on a thin sleeping mat, shaking with fear. I knew that the god of thunder had the power to kill me. A god that could enable a grown woman to sit in a burning fire—and thunder!—would not be bothered by a small boy. My life now seemed as insignificant to me as the lamp in the corner of my room. It was only a tin can with a small wick sticking out of a punctured hole, and while it gave off tremendous smoke, there was far more darkness than light. I watched the wick slowly flicker out and as I curled up on the floor, looking like a covered termite hill with my single backcloth, I shed tears. I no longer cared if I learned to read. I only wanted to be home in Banga, on the shores of Lake Victoria.

The next morning I rose early and walked to school

with the other village children. I was shy and did not
expose my tears, but I was still afraid. At any moment
I expected lightning to fall from the sky and strike me
dead. When we finally arrived at the school yard I
breathed a sigh of relief. A bell rang and I followed the
other children into a large mud building with a corrugated iron roof. We assembled in a hall and I noticed that
everyone seemed to have a friend except myself. The
boys were dressed in white shirts and khaki shorts; the
girls in khaki dresses with white ribbons across their
chests. I supposed that none of them came from a village
as poor and small as Banga. The headmaster was a tall
stately man by the name of Nambuli and he was dressed
humbly in khaki shorts. He directed the students to sing
"Rock of Ages," but because I did not know the words
I was silent. When the song was finally over Nambuli
commanded everyone to shut his eyes.

"We will speak now to the Father in heaven," he said.

I looked around the room and saw everyone closing
their eyes, except for a few "green ones" like myself.
Nambuli said, "In Jesus' name," and the whole room
sounded "Amen." It all happened very quickly but for
me it was a moment of great discovery. I had not known
that I myself could talk to God.

That afternoon I walked home alone, talking to the
Father in heaven. I told Him of the threat against my life
and asked Him to protect me from the god of thunder.
Afterwards I played outdoors with the other village children and from that day on we walked home from school
together, playing and laughing. It was only when I saw
clouds gathering in the sky that I went off to be by
myself. At such times I would pray to God, telling Him
of my fear and asking for His protection.

I lived in the home of the shrine priestess for three
years, going back to Banga only for vacations. At home

I often read the Bible to my mother but by then she was not as interested in the teachings of Jesus as she was in the way I made words out of marks on paper.

When I returned from these times with my family the shrine priestess would renew her challenge: "If your God is so powerful, why don't you come sit with me in the fire? Then we will see who serves the true God!"

Now, 20 years later, as a university professor and minister of a large church, I was hearing the challenge again. I looked at the healed boy and his mother, and at the witch doctor still lying at my feet. A deep suspicion overcame me. Perhaps they too had come only to mock my faith and bring disrepute to the gospel.

My fears came to nothing. While still kneeling, the witch doctor repeated her request and in the midst of my confusion I felt the prompting of the Spirit. After some hesitation, I explained to the witch doctor that she could have the power of Jesus Christ but only for a great price—she must first surrender her own powers. To my surprise, the woman agreed immediately. She was ready to give up everything, she claimed, to become a part of God's Kingdom. All she needed to know was what it was that she should do.

This public boldness convinced me of the witch's sincerity. I put my hand on her shoulder and prayed for her, that God would give her the power of Jesus Christ. When I said "Amen," the witch doctor rose to her feet and bowed with great dignity. She thanked me for her new power and asked for an appointment on the following Thursday. On that day, she promised, she was going to bring her gods and fetishes to the churchyard, and she was going to burn them all.

We said good-bye and while I walked to the pulpit, the witch doctor went to find a seat on the far side of the compound. During the singing, and even as I was preaching, I often found my eyes wandering to the spot where I assumed she was sitting. *Would the woman really come to burn her fetishes?* I wondered. I had never heard of a witch giving up her powers. A compromise of sworn allegiance to Satan and his kingdom meant instant death; no witch could surrender her craft and hope to live. And even if she did trust in God's power for her preservation, there were many other things she stood to lose. The woman was a prominent witch in Kampala and her witchcraft was not only her religion, but her income and prestige as well. If she gave up the gods, she would be giving up her whole life.

The following Monday I met with five elders from the church for prayer. We agreed to continue praying and fasting until the burning, and we met together for prayer several more times. Late Thursday afternoon, the witch doctor drove her bright blue minibus into the church-yard. When she unlatched the back doors and opened them wide, I could hardly believe the sight. The van was packed with hundreds of sacred articles. There were brightly colored backcloths, spears and shields, old coins, and dozens of polished sticks twisted into peculiar shapes. The witch unloaded the fetishes one by one and placed them in a pile under a nearby tree. Last of all, she took out a large cylinder of canvas which had been embroidered with beads and cowrie shells. She placed the cylinder on top of the pile and then stepped back with a solemn air.

The elders and I gathered with the witch around the pile, and one of the elders asked about the cylinder.

"It is the likeness of the god from whom I receive my power," the witch explained. "It is the god of thunder."

My legs went weak as she said the name. It was the god who had once threatened to kill me. For a moment I felt again the deep fear I had known as a small boy walking through the swamp to Kiyoola Primary School. I heard again the shrill curses of the shrine priestess, and from deep within me my heart cried to God. Even now, 20 years later, I knew the vows of the priestess were strong enough to destroy us all.

The elders and I made a circle to pray and for a moment no one spoke. From childhood we each had lived with the same deep fear of the gods and now the long confident prayers of the past three days disappeared in the face of the threatening pile of images and fetishes. None of us wanted a direct confrontation with the demonic.

Finally I myself said a brief prayer. When I finished, one of the elders passed me a box of matches. In the quiet conversation that followed I passed them to another, but he in turn passed them on to his neighbor. In seconds the matches had gone from hand to hand and were back in my own. I could almost feel the accusing eyes of the elders: "You are the one who preaches the gospel, now you be the one to demonstrate it!"

I hesitated and then I set fire to the sacred objects. In a few minutes, the entire demonic kingdom was in flames. The elders and the witch and I stood and watched the burning for almost an hour, and our fears disappeared. In their place was a new jubilation. The kindled fire seemed as the holy anger of God and the acrid odor coming from the burning objects smelled like the sweet aroma of freedom. When the pile finally was reduced to ashes, the witch wept and shouted for joy. The elders and I joined in her rejoicing and thanked God for rescuing one of Satan's own servants from the kingdom of darkness.

After the burning service, an elder and I took the witch aside and explained to her the consequences of her freedom. God had given her the power for which she had asked, now she must give to Him her life. I read to her from God's Word, and she listened carefully. When she understood that Jesus Christ had died for her sins and had made it possible for her to be a member of God's own Kingdom, she wept again. She confessed her sins and received Jesus as her new Lord.

On the following Sunday, the converted witch came to church and spoke of her deliverance before the entire congregation.

"Satan cares nothing for his devotees," she explained, "except to use them and to destroy them. His devotees are called *omukongozi*, 'those who carry the king on their backs,' and they know their fate in advance. They chant in the voice of their god, 'When I kill you, I will possess another,' and they sing in their choruses, 'They will burn me along with a multitude of children.'

"It is a wonder," the converted witch concluded, "when a boy's leg is healed and it is a wonder when a devotee throws away the gods and lives. But it is no wonder when a witch sits in the fire. The fire is the home of the devil and he allows all of his students to sit with him."

Before the witch doctor had finished speaking the church compound started humming with the sounds of celebration. The choir burst into song, and the congregation began clapping and dancing for joy. It was a moment of great triumph, a day when Jesus' words took on a new meaning for us all:

> But if I with the finger of God cast out devils, no doubt the kingdom of God is come upon you.[9]

7

You Are Burning Us

The news of the witch doctor's conversion spread rapidly throughout Kampala and its neighboring towns. The woman's prominence had come not only from her skill as a witch doctor but from her function as an "officiator," one who initiates other devotees into the profession, and many of her former disciples and fellow workers began attending church services. They came to learn of the new power which their colleague had discovered. After hearing the gospel, many left their old gods and became followers of Jesus Christ, and by December of 1972 we had baptized over 150 witch doctors. Each convert attended a burning service in the churchyard. There, where the first "burning" had taken place, thousands of gods and fetishes were put to the fire.

It was during this time that a strange event took place in the home of one of Kampala's most prominent and wealthy families. One day after a particularly large baptismal service I was meeting with two elders in the vestry of the church, discussing the growth of our congregation. We had been talking for some time about the need for a "small group" ministry when we were interrupted by a well-dressed middle-aged man who rushed through the door without knocking. His clothes were in complete disarray, and he looked as if he had not slept for several days. "Sebo, please come quickly!" he cried. "My mother has shut her mouth and is soon to die. Please come and pray for her! Pray so that she will die in peace with a Christian blessing!"

I did not recognize the man, but in Baganda society, when someone "shuts his mouth" he stops talking and eating. It is the sign that death is near. I knew that he was asking me to pronounce last rites over his mother. It was a practice customary only among Roman Catholics and I hesitated to involve myself. I told the man that I would be with him after I had consulted with the elders, but he refused to accept a delay.

"My mother is about to collapse," he shouted. "She doesn't have time for your consultations!"

The family lived on the west slope of Makerere Hill. I arrived at their dwelling with two elders and recognized it immediately as belonging to Kampala's most famous merchant family. A large crowd of mourners had gathered on the front lawn around an open fire. They were weeping and moaning and when they recognized me as "the clergy," their lamentations became even louder.

Inside, the scene was the same. The house was packed with family members waiting for the woman to give her last breath. As I followed the son to the bedroom one

75

old woman grabbed my sleeve and cried, "O Lord, may she die quickly and go in peace!" Like the other mourners, her face was stained with tears and her waist garments were tied tightly around her body. For a moment I was overcome with the sights and sounds of death.

The woman was lying on a large mahogany bed in her richly furnished bedroom. Over the bed was a mosquito net and, although the light was dim, I was able to see her face. It was an attractive face, but it was already turning gray and seemed worn and wasted. Her eyes were shut gently, as if death had already come.

When I stepped to her bed, I was surprised to see the woman tremble. In seconds she was shaking violently and sweating. With strange twists of her body she slammed herself against the wall and in a harsh male voice she cried out for help. "The destroyer is here!" she shrieked. "You are the ones who are burning us!"

The woman's cries puzzled me and astonished her family. They had not heard her speak for days and now, just as she was dying, strange sentences that no one could understand were coming from her mouth. I waited as the family members calmed themselves and then, when the woman had finished shaking, I laid my hand on her head. I asked God to receive her into His Kingdom and to comfort her.

I finished praying and there was a moment of silence. Then the sick woman opened her eyes and, taking my hand in her own, she sat up in bed. Her sheets were soaked in perspiration and she was breathing heavily, but her eyes were clear. She looked around the room and, in an exhausted voice, she asked a member of the family to bring some tea. No one moved to help her. Everyone was paralyzed with astonishment. Those who only a few minutes before had no words for the dying now suddenly found themselves without words for the living. Finally, one young woman dashed from the room and ran throughout the house shouting the good news. The crowd of mourners hummed in astonishment and then broke into loud rejoicing. Someone brought tea and we all stood around the woman's bed, watching her drink her tea, and feeling awkward. The healed woman said nothing but only stared at us, her eyes wide in wonder.

The elders and I left the family by themselves as soon as possible and all the way back to the churchyard we puzzled over the healing of the woman, and her strange cries. In the tension of the moment I myself had not understood what she was saying. When the elders told me, I was only more puzzled. What could she have meant? How could we be burning her? Was she referring to our burning services for witch doctors? It seemed unlikely. None of us ever had any contact with the woman before, and neither she nor any members of her family attended the Redeemed Church.

The cries of the wealthy woman remained a mystery until the following Sunday. On that day, she and her entire family attended church and gave public praises to God. After the service, in conversation with her son, I learned that just days before her illness the woman had consulted with a witch doctor concerning a domestic affair. It was startling news and it was only then I understood her deathbed shout, "You are the ones who are burning us!" It was the cry of one possessed.

The enormity of this knowledge overwhelmed me and, for the first time in my life, I began to understand the scope of Satan's kingdom. It was a kingdom of innumerable loyal subjects, whose shrines were not only inanimate objects but human beings themselves. No matter how many fetishes we burned and no matter how many witches were converted, we would never reduce the number of demons. These deeply committed servants of Satan, communicating and invisible members of a spiritual network of evil, could not be fought by flesh and blood.

I was reminded of my own childhood experiences, of Okelo and his paralyzed arms, of the boy with the lame leg, of the hundreds of converted witch doctors. I thought of the man standing before me, of his mother and her deathbed struggle. We were all people who once had been overcome by Satan and the solidarity of evil. The kingdom of darkness had invaded our lives with power, but in Jesus Christ, the Kingdom of God had triumphed.

A few weeks after the healing of the wealthy woman, on a Monday afternoon in late December, a leading witch doctor in Kampala, Kiganira Omumbaale cursed the Redeemed Church.

"Soon," he announced to a large gathering of his disciples, "these people of God will be destroyed. Kefa Sempangi is going to die a miserable death. I have said it."

Two days later the night watchman at the church notified the committee of elders that a band of witches had visited the compound where we worshiped. They came, he said, at three in the morning and made a large circle around the pulpit. After dancing and performing many sacrilegious and obscene rites, they sprinkled a fine white powder over the grounds. Then they disappeared into the night.

The watchman's news caused deep concern among many of the elders. Kiganira Omumbaale, which means "Kiganira the witch doctor," was a prominent citizen in Kampala and he was known to have tremendous powers. Two years before Uganda's independence from Great Britain he had prophesied, while hanging from a tree limb, that the Baganda king would soon return from exile. The Baganda king, Mutesa II, had been exiled by Great Britain, and Kiganira made his prophecy at a time when churches in Uganda prayed only for the Queen of England. He was soon imprisoned for his statement, but two years later independence came. King Mutesa II returned from exile, and from that time on Kiganira's power was complete. Thousands of people from all over Uganda came to receive *baraka*, blessings, from his hands, and he soon had a larger following than any witch doctor in Kampala. His success led him to ask President Obote, in the first years of his government, to make witchcraft the national religion of Uganda. Obote refused, but Kiganira had made his point.

Now, in response to the witch doctor's new prophecy, the elders of the church called an all-night prayer meeting. The meeting was packed with concerned church members reminding themselves of God's protection. I too attended the prayer, but I felt little alarm. I had learned in recent months that God's power was a direct response to Satan's kingdom, and I knew that neither the witch doctor nor his gods had any power over my life.

On the Saturday following the prayer meeting, Kiganira went with his wife to Lake Nalubaale to practice his rituals. He floated out to the middle of the lake in an inner tube, as was his custom, and he sat in such a way as to appear to be sitting on the water. Then he began to address his followers and bestow blessings upon the many people who had come to seek his favor.

What happened next was never clearly understood. For some reason the witch doctor slipped from his tube and disappeared from sight. Moments of anxious searching followed, but it was only hours later that his drowned body was recovered.

The news of Kiganira's death brought great rejoicing to the congregation of the Redeemed Church and marked the end of open satanic opposition to our ministry. While witch doctors and their craft continued to grow in popularity under the regime of Idi Amin—who was said to openly practice human blood rituals—we never again experienced as a church a direct attack from the gods. But, unknown to us, Satan was already preparing a new and even more strategic attack.

8

I Need a Vono Bed

On February 13, 1972, Idi Amin made a short trip to Libya. Before he returned, Uganda's 10-year friendship with Israel had ended and a new relationship with the Arab nations had begun.

In Libya, Amin convinced Colonel Qadhafi and other Arab leaders that Uganda was a Muslim nation. Eighty percent of Uganda's 11 million people, Amin claimed, followed Mohammed and were suppressed by a small Christian minority. They could be liberated with help from their Muslim allies, the Arab people. Leaders from Libya and Saudi Arabia believed Amin's lies—Muslims are only six percent of Uganda's population—and pledged financial support. Libya alone contributed over 30 million dollars "to eliminate the few remaining Christians and turn Uganda to a Muslim state."[10] The money came from the *Jihad*, "Holy War" Fund.

By late 1972, Amin's campaign of terror against Catholics and Protestants was well underway. In the army there were bloody massacres and forced conversions. In the civil sector there were thousands of "disappearances." Many of those killed were men and women who had revealed their education and financial assets in government applications which were ostensibly designed to find new owners for abandoned Asian businesses. A government security committee blamed this outbreak of killings on guerrilla activity. Supporters of former President Milton Obote, they charged, were trying to undermine the free government of Uganda. Zionists and imperialists were trying to sabotage Amin's "economic" war.

In the last three months of 1972, while the western world dismissed stories of genocide as wild exaggerations by frightened refugees, Idi Amin and his soldiers killed over 90,000 Ugandans. By December there was hardly a prominent family left in Uganda which had not experienced the brutal killing of one of its members.

One Sunday in December, just before the start of our afternoon service, four men hurried into the vestry of the Redeemed Church, carrying a sick woman on a stretcher. Close behind them were the relatives of the woman, weeping and crying out in distress. One of the women in the group of mourners shouted, "Help us! Help us!" in a hysterical and desperate voice. Another woman was carrying a small child not more than two years old. The child was sucking on her thumb and staring vacantly around the room. Later I learned that she was the infant daughter of the woman on the stretcher.

The elders and I were gathered in the vestry for prayer and the men laid the stretcher down in the middle of our circle. The woman was tied to the stretcher by three straps and her face was swollen and green. It seemed as if she had already lost a great deal of blood and I could see ugly black bruises covering her neck. Her eyes were fixed in a vacant stare and her body was completely stiff. When I saw that she was paralyzed I knew that she did not belong in our church vestry. She needed immediate medical attention.

I looked helplessly down at the woman, and one of the men who carried her into the room began telling her story. She was a woman of Lukuli, an exclusive village on the western edge of Kampala, and her husband was a wealthy and noble man. Three days earlier, in the middle of the day, Amin's soldiers came to their home. They had rounded up the family and herded them into one room, and then they seized the husband. In front of his family, they forced the man to drink his wife's urine. Then they cut him with bayonets, and fed him his own flesh. Finally they slashed off his hands and, as he died twisting and turning in his own blood, they raped his wife.

The soldiers plundered the house completely and, pleased with the success of their raid, they climbed, laughing and joking, into an army van. The situation they left behind was hopeless. The head of the household, the lion of the family, had been destroyed. All taboos had been broken, and the shame and suffering inflicted on the family was complete. In utter despair, the new widow turned her back on her children and with her last physical effort, attempted to strangle herself.

"She passed out before she suffocated," the man said, finishing his story in the same flat voice with which he had begun it. "And now we have brought her to you." He looked at me expectantly. I saw in his face and in the faces of those standing around him a firm conviction. *These people*, I thought, *think I can heal their friend. They think the gospel is a magic formula, like witchcraft.* For a moment my sense of helplessness turned to anger and I wished I could bodily evict everyone from the vestry. Trying to remain calm, I directed the men who had carried the stretcher into the room to carry it out.

"Take your friend to a hospital," I said. "She needs professional help. We are not doctors here, we are preachers of the Word. There is no way I can diagnose her illness."

There was complete silence until an elderly woman standing quietly in the background suddenly spoke up. She was angry. She addressed me with an uncompromising voice and gathered herself up stiffly in indignation. "Do you think," she said, "that when people brought their sick friends to Jesus they didn't know where the hospital was?"

The woman's anger intimidated me and I did not know how to respond. I turned for help to Kiwanuka who had been watching the whole affair with an interested eye. Since his conversion Kiwanuka had become not only my close friend but a respected counselor and confidant as well. I knew that he would help me now. I knew that he could convince the people to leave. They were men and women from his own class and Kiwanuka always knew exactly how to speak with them, even in the most difficult situations.

But when Kiwanuka pulled me aside, his words were for me, not for the others. "Kefa," he said in his most aggressive manner, "we have baptized over 150 witch doctors. What business have we destroying the people's doctors if we don't know what to do with their sick?"

Kiwanuka's remarks left me feeling betrayed and more helpless than ever. Was he thinking, just as the others, that the gospel was magic? Did he think that the Holy Spirit could be manipulated by mere men? I had no formulas with which to heal the woman. And I was not like the great prophets and preachers of the past. I was not like Elijah or Samuel, Peter or Paul. I had no special access to God. Besides, I continued arguing with myself, the woman could die at any moment. What would people think and say when they heard that the pastor of the Redeemed Church had kept a dying woman from the hospital?

With this last thought, I was convicted of my own self-concern and foolishness. I was reminded of the child Okelo and of the work God had done in his life. It was not I who had delivered him, but the strong words of Jesus Christ, the same Christ who said, "I can do nothing of myself, but the Father in me, He does the works."[11] I too could do nothing of myself. But, like Paul, I could do everything through the power of the resurrected Lord.

I turned again to the relatives and this time I asked them to sit down. I took my Bible and stood over the sick woman's stretcher. For more than an hour I read to her from the book of John. When it was time for the service, another elder took my place and continued with the reading. I returned after the service and the woman was still lying unconscious. She had not moved once since she had been brought into the vestry. I could see the disappointment on the faces of her friends and relatives. *They have heard incredible stories of instant healings*, I said to myself. *They have heard of the lame leaving the churchyard leaping. Now their expectations are disappointed. The woman they have brought into the church will leave the same way she came—on a stretcher.*

We kept the woman in the vestry for the remainder of the day and throughout the night. She slipped in and

85

out of consciousness, and she often moaned or tried to twist her body out of the straps. Whenever she awakened, there was an elder at her side reading to her of the Resurrection and of God's love for His suffering people.

By morning the woman was completely conscious and able to sit up in a chair. Her face was still swollen but she had almost regained her normal coloring. Before long she recovered her voice and her first questions were of her children. She spoke of each one by name and then shuddering and weeping, she told the story of the shameful terror they had been forced to witness.

"That is why I could not bear to live," she said in an exhausted, broken voice. "I could not bear that my children had seen their father suffer such things."

My heart went out to the woman as she relived her nightmarish experience. I knew that the training and expectations of those raised in her privileged position were much different than the expectations of the villagers with whom I had spent my childhood. In our villages we lived at the edge of the precipice; each new day brought new fears and insecurities, new suffering. Violent torturous deaths either at the hands of wild animals or human enemies were not uncommon. But for city people such sufferings were known only from stories. And this woman sitting before me, I knew, had no categories in which to place events that were beyond the ability of human beings to comprehend and endure.

I prayed with the woman for a long time, asking God to bring His peace and healing to her life. When I finished, a neighbor who had spent the night in the vestry came forward to take her home to her relatives. The woman rose weakly and seemed about to collapse. Then she gathered her strength and, holding tightly to her neighbor's arm, she walked out the door. As I watched her leave, I felt tears fall down my cheeks. She seemed to me to be so frail and I wondered if she would ever recover from the terrible wounds she had suffered.

In the following week several elders visited with the woman and reported back to the committee of elders on her favorable progress. I myself heard nothing of the woman until two Sundays later when she came to church accompanied by her children and her friends and her relatives. They all sat together on the front row and with my first glance at the woman I could see that what the elders had said was true. The woman seemed to be completely well. Her face not only had returned to its normal shape but was healthy and glowing. She sat in her chair with confidence and strength and seemed to be the center of courage for the entire family. After the service, she led her family and friends forward to hear the message of salvation and together they committed their lives to Jesus Christ.

I was astonished by the woman's recovery and the conversion of her family. I turned to Kiwanuka to share my amazement with him but he only looked at me and laughed. He stretched out his arms as if to say, what else could it be? Then he began praising God in a loud voice. "This Man Jesus!" he said, "What a Man He is! Whatever He says must come to pass!" I realized then that Kiwanuka, the most complex human being I had ever met, had a most simple faith. He stood firmly on the foundation of God's Word with no lingering doubts undermining his convictions. Whatever he read in the Bible he believed to be true. For him, God was so real, and whatever God said must come to pass.

Word of the woman's healing spread rapidly and in the weeks that followed, we of the Redeemed Church experienced a special visitation from God. Dozens of widows and orphans, their lives shattered by Amin's rampaging soldiers, were brought to the church for prayer. Again and again, in the presence of the most excruciating human grief and sorrow, we witnessed the power of God's healing love. Destroyed minds and bodies were restored, and out of gratitude hundreds committed their lives to the service of Jesus Christ.

During this time, the elders and I began to talk among ourselves of beginning a counseling center to meet the needs of the many emotionally and spiritually troubled people we were encountering through the work of the church. One day as we sat in the vestry and discussed plans for sending some of our number abroad for professional training in counseling, we were interrupted by an urgent knock at the door. One of the elders opened the door and there stood a tall thin woman dressed in ragged gray clothes. She was barefoot and her hair was not properly combed, but she seemed totally unashamed in our presence. I could see in her face the erosions of extreme poverty and I also saw that while she was almost defeated, she had not yet given up.

"I have come to ask you to pray," she said in a desperate voice. "I am so much in need of a vono bed and there is no way I can get one. God has to provide for me."

A vono bed! I could hardly believe my ears. A vono bed was nothing but a mattress with springs. It was true that for the poor such a mattress was a luxury—most of them slept on the floor with straw mats—but I had never heard anyone making a simple mattress an urgent matter for prayer. It seemed especially strange now, when our whole country was in serious trouble. God was doing a mighty work in our midst. Surely we all had more pressing things to think about!

One of the elders promised that we would pray for the bed and after many reassurances the woman left the room. I immediately forgot her request and was surprised when, during our prayer time, several elders remembered the woman's mattress. The whole matter seemed to me even more trivial than ever and I was glad when we moved on to other things. After the meeting we stepped from the vestry and the woman was waiting for us at the door. She demanded to know if we had prayed for her bed. I assured her that we had, but I could hardly keep the irritation from my voice. The woman appeared not to notice that I was annoyed. She only thanked me and went her way.

The following Sunday the woman was in church making a big commotion. I sent an usher to inquire into the trouble and he returned several minutes later with the woman at his side. Her face was shining and she was almost dancing with excitement. When she saw me standing among the crowd she shouted, "The Kingdom of God has come! The Kingdom of God has come! Jesus has given me a vono bed!"

I nodded my head and smiled at the woman to show my appreciation for her answered prayer, but I did not inquire any further into her story. I was curious as to how she had found a mattress but we were standing near the area where many of the prominent members of the church were seated. I did not want to encourage the woman in her excessive excitement or to identify myself with her own simplistic understanding of the gospel.

Despite this quick dismissal, the memory of the woman's excitement remained with me for many days. "The Kingdom of God has come! Jesus has given me a vono bed!" I wondered if it was true. Did the coming of the Kingdom have something to do with the fact that this poor woman was no longer sleeping on rags but on a mattress? And if so, what?

I began to listen with new ears to the prayers of petition and thanksgiving coming from members of the congregation. We had a long sharing-time before each service and we were receiving over 200 letters a week from people whose lives had been touched by God at our services. In both verbal and written testimonies, the same message was repeated over and over again. God was meeting the needs of His children. He was blessing them not only with spiritual gifts and physical healings, but with increased crops, fair prices, reconciled relationships, and pregnancies. In marriages, on the farm, at jobs—there was seemingly no activity of life too insignificant to be touched by His grace.

These testimonies caused me to read again the story of Jesus' earthly ministry. The more I read and reflected on His life, the more I saw the naked inadequacy of my own approach to the gospel. *I* met people at my point of expertise, my knowledge of the Scripture. *Christ* met people at their point of need. When a blind man asked Him to restore his eyes, Jesus did not give him religion. He gave him his sight. It was only later that He paid a second visit to give the man the message of salvation.

I thought of the poor woman and her vono bed. Her problem was perhaps not as serious as the blind man's but her experience of God's grace was the same. She had heard the gospel not as abstract concepts but as concrete promises, and when she had been in need of a mattress, she looked to God. God used her need to communicate His love. Now, when night came to Kampala, there would be many people sleeping on beds but perhaps only one woman who slept on a bed which had manifested God's glory.

This realization brought with it a new understanding of the importance of witchcraft among my people. We were, I knew, a needy people. We could not afford to be answered in abstractions. We could not afford to separate doctrine and life. Even our language reflects this need for the concrete. "Truth" for a non-westernized

African does not refer to a statement's correspondence with a fact. Truth is a quality of *things*. A mango tree is true if it bears sweet mangoes, a house is true if it is upright. A man is true if he knows how to meet difficult situations without losing his head, if he knows how to run his home, control his temper, resist gossip.

A religion is true if it *works*, if it meets *all* the needs of the people. A religion that speaks only to man's soul and not to his body is not true. Africans make no distinction between the spiritual and the physical. The spiritual is not a category among categories but the lens through which all of life is viewed. A tribesman from my village knows that cutting a tree, climbing a mountain, making a fire, planting a garden and bowing before the gods are all religious acts. He lives in the presence of the gods, and he knows that without intervention from them, without *baraka*, a blessing, there is nothing. There is no coffee harvest, no wood for the fire, no wife, no children.

For such people, people who live their lives in daily hardship at the edge of nothingness, witchcraft is not a set of beliefs. It is a way of life. I have never heard a poor or needy person discuss the philosophy of witchcraft. Their only concern is what it does, that it works. A well-educated Ugandan once told me, speaking of his visits to a witch doctor, "I know it is diabolical, but at least it is substantial." A young lady, trying desperately to recover from a nervous breakdown, told me that if God could not help her mental instability she knew a goddess who could. At the time I found these remarks offensive, but now I understood that both of these people had one thing in common: they were needy people. They were not looking for a world view but for a power to transform their lives. If Christianity could not help them, the witch doctor could.

It was a lesson my father had tried to teach me many years before. In my first year as a student at University of Makerere I led dozens of student evangelism teams in street meetings throughout Kampala. The meetings were tremendously successful and this work of grace in the lives of strangers gave me a burning desire to return to my family and see my father saved. I wrote him numerous letters from Kampala about the judgment of God upon his life and his need to repent.

I returned to my father's home during the long vacation at the end of my school term. My mother had died in 1962 from a pregnancy complication, and shortly afterwards my father and many other family members left the village of Banga. Now they were living and farming in Nyize, a small remote village 70 miles east of Kampala.

I arrived at Nyize in the middle of the cotton harvest. My father greeted me with a sack in his hand and after a short welcome we went into the fields. Each morning we rose early and spent the day picking and cleaning cotton. As we worked, we spent long hours in silence and long hours in conversation. We talked about the village, my mother, the price of cotton, the new ways that came from the city. We told riddles and exchanged proverbs. My father was a man of dignity, a village subchief, and I was honored to work by his side. But I never spoke the message I had brought from Kampala. I had grown too accustomed to shouting from a distance and now, face to face, I had nothing to say.

Three times a week, in the late afternoon, I left my father to go to the village bazaar and proclaim the gospel. It was only a small market with six or seven shops but during the cotton season it was crowded with people. There were farmers in dusty work clothes carrying sacks of cotton to the ginnery scales, and there were merchants peddling cooking oil, maize flour, salt and sweet breads. There were shopkeepers with tin pans and clay pots. It was these people to whom I preached and there was always a large crowd, including dogs, goats and chickens, to listen to my message.

The response was good. The villagers were eager to hear the words of salvation and the grace of God touched many lives. But as I stood in the middle of the bazaar confessing my sins and sharing the good news of redemption I often found myself hoping my father would come to hear me. I wanted him to find the grace I had found, I wanted him to know Jesus.

He never came. Our home was only a few houses from the bazaar, and sometimes just as I started to preach he would walk past the crowd on his way to visit my grandmother. But he never stopped and he never appeared to listen. I watched him go with a sad heart. Why did God soften the hearts of the villagers and not the heart of my own father? Why did He not answer my prayers?

One evening, just as the sun was setting on the village, I returned home tired but happy. I had preached for over three hours and there had been many responses. My father commented on the large crowd he had seen at the bazaar and I explained to him the success of my message. Many people in our village were becoming Christians. The power of God was being made known. Soon the entire village would be transformed.

When I finished speaking my father was quiet for a long time. Finally he spoke. "Son," he said, "think of the women who listen to you in the bazaar. There is one woman who quarrels with her husband almost every evening. Can your words change her?"

I started to explain the power of God but my father was not finished. "Think of the husband. He toils in the field the whole day long to bring two small bags of

93

cotton to the market. He rides on a broken bicycle. He stands in a long line. In the end he is cheated by the false weights of dishonest Asian merchants. He takes his money and looks without hope at the goods sold in the market. There are cotton shirts, cotton dresses, cotton mats and shoes. Maybe he is looking at cotton he has picked with his own hands. But he cannot own a cotton shirt. The little he has will never be enough. He buys a few kilos of meat and goes home empty-handed. He quarrels with his wife and beats his children. There is no money in the home for the rest of the year. There is no peace and there is no joy. What do your words have to do with him?"

My father walked to the doorway of our home and pointed to the hill whose shadow was beginning to fall over the village.

"At the top of the hill," he said, "lives the god of the village Nyize. It is from him that we take our name. *Nyize* means 'I am furious.' When the drought comes, we know Nyize is angry. We take food and beer to the python on the hill. We sit on the grass in front of his cave and make our fire. We drum and sing and dance and put eggs in front of his cave. When the python comes to eat, we know he has accepted our sacrifice.

"It is then we celebrate in thanksgiving. We slaughter our goats and our chickens. We offer their blood to Nyize and roast their flesh for eating. Whoever offers blood makes a wish." My father stopped and was quiet for a minute.

"I knew a man once," he continued, "who wanted to become a chief. He sacrificed three goats to Nyize. Now he is the head of the Muluka. And there are many other cases. Barren women become mothers, bachelors find wives, and cotton and coffee fields prosper."

I was discouraged by my father's words. I did not see

94

how they related to the good news I was preaching and I thought to myself. *It is no use speaking anymore. He is evading the challenge of my message. He has no ears for the gospel of Jesus Christ.*

I looked at the floor, hoping my father would see I was unhappy and inquire about my sadness. Then I would share with him my message.

But my father went on speaking. "I knew another man," he said, "who was a follower of Jesus Christ. He went to church every Sunday. He did not drink banana beer. When his flock of sheep became sick, the church said nothing to him. He went to the witch doctor to buy a blessing. Now his flock is the biggest in the village."

My father stopped and looked at me. He saw I had not yet understood his message, and he wanted me to know its meaning.

"The man still goes to church," he said. "He is like your converts. They go to church on Sunday. But when they need someone to stand between their flocks and death, they will know where to go. In such times men do not need words, they need power."

When he finished we sat in silence for a long time. I knew my father's words were true. Men and women of the bush mixed their faith in Jesus Christ with the practice of witchcraft. They visited the pastor of their church on Sunday, but on Monday they went to see the witch doctor. It was the witch doctor they trusted with the affairs of everyday life. It was he who arranged their marriages, who settled their quarrels and guaranteed their harvest. But what could this sad situation have to do with the message I was preaching? The native gods had a strong hold on village life because villagers were uneducated. They did not know about science and the success of western technology. They did not know about agriculture and modern medicine. Their world was full of experiences which could not be explained, and I was not surprised to find that their Christian faith revealed ignorance. It would be several generations before the fruit of the Spirit could be seen clearly.

With these thoughts I hid myself from my father's wisdom. I did not have ears to hear his concern for the poor and I did not hear him ask, "What does Jesus have to do with the sufferings of my people?

"Human beings are creatures with many needs," he had tried to say. "There are human beings with needs so deep they cannot hear your doctrine. They are creatures who need food, rain, honest wages, good marriages. They need a god who is concerned with the details of their lives. If the gospel you are preaching does not speak to human needs, it is useless. It cannot compete with the witch doctor and the gods."

The memory of my father's words and my experience with the vono-bed woman brought a new and sobering understanding to my life. The kingdom of darkness had invaded every area of our existence. The death and destruction we were experiencing in Uganda was only one of Satan's means of destroying men, but no activity of life left him unconcerned. He was ready to use the smallest of human needs to communicate himself to mankind and gain control over God's creation. At the same time, at every point where Satan was strong, the redemptive power of Jesus Christ was stronger. Christ had reconciled *all* things to Himself. It was in understanding the holistic gospel where we as Ugandan Christians had failed. We had witnessed God's Kingdom as a direct power against the kingdom of darkness in the everyday activities of our lives. We had gone many times to the homes of the poor and received a cup of tea from their hands, and then opened our Bibles to give them spiritual tranquilizers. We had not seen the miserable conditions of their existence as part of Satan's dominion. We had not shared with them the good news that the same gospel that empowers men for conversion, empowers them to overcome their economic poverty.

Similar mistakes had been repeated in politics. It was customary among Christians in Uganda to pray for good leaders. At the same time, if a believer announced his intentions to pursue a political career, all-night prayers were called on his behalf. Surely no one would choose a career in politics unless he was "backsliding"! Kiwanuka was the one person I knew who had ignored these pressures from the Christian community. After his conversion, almost all his Christian friends had encouraged him to leave behind his political affiliations. Kiwanuka only pursued them more vigorously. "God has made men to be political animals," he would say, "and I for one am going to be a man!"

Now I wondered if the Christian community itself didn't bear some responsibility for the reign of Idi Amin. In any case, clearly it was time for the church to move in a new direction. If Christ's redemption was holistic, then the message we preached must speak to the whole of human existence.

I shared this conviction with the committee of elders in January of 1973 and we began to make plans for broadening the ministry to the church. We would, we agreed, equip ourselves to meet Satan at every point of attack. We determined to send abroad qualified people from our midst for training in theology, business management, printing, agriculture and social work. We would begin to teach our people that the church was not simply a reservoir, but a channel of God's blessing. We would emphasize the holistic nature of redemption and begin as a church to make visible the concrete promises of God.

Our vision for our future ministry was not dampened but only strengthened by Amin's reign of terror. It seemed to us that his reign would be short. His enemies now numbered in the hundreds of thousands and already there had been several attempts on his life. It would not be long before there was a successful *coup* or some foreign country intervened on our behalf. Until that time, we were willing to wait—and pray.

9
Give Us the Gun!

In early February of 1973 there was a new wave of killings in Kampala. Amin and his advisors drew up a list of 2,000 prominent Ugandans—professors, businessmen, church leaders, government officials and others—and scheduled them for execution. Ten squads of assassins, largely Nubians from the brutal State Research Bureau, were commissioned to hunt the victims down.

The pattern of arrests was almost always the same. The Nubian assassins, dressed in their "uniform" of sunglasses, flowered shirts and bell-bottom trousers, entered an office or home in broad daylight. They called out the name of their victim and humiliated him in front of employees and family members. The terrified man was then tied up and dragged away to the trunk of a waiting automobile. His screams for help meant nothing. No one dared to lend a hand.

Only a few victims were killed immediately. The rest were taken to prison and tortured to death by the most sadistic methods. Some were cut with bayonets and made to eat their own flesh. Some were thrown into deep pits of freezing water and fed only enough for a slow agonizing death. Others had arms, legs or genitals cut off and were left in the dirt to bleed to death. Women were raped and their reproductive organs set on fire. In one prison, Naguru College, men were tricked into killing each other. A prisoner was given a heavy hammer and promised freedom if he would smash in the head of another. When after many blows his fellow prisoner died, another prisoner was brought to the courtyard, with the same promise of freedom, to kill the "executioner" with the same hammer. The chain went on for hours. Soldiers and Nubians gathered in the courtyard to watch the bloody spectacle. They drank gin, and laughed and joked. When the killings were quick and merciful, they cursed in anger. When they were slow and torturous, they rejoiced. Their hearts were knit together in a terrible celebration of death and suffering.

The bodies of Amin's first victims had been buried in mass graves. Later they were thrown into the river or burned with petrol fires. Now, dozens of bodies were simply left to rot, unburied, in the streets of Kampala. Even the thick stone walls of Makerere University could not keep out the dead. More than once I passed mutilated and discarded bodies on my way to the classroom.

One day in January of 1973 I attended a meeting of the university fine arts department to discuss with my colleagues a five-year development plan. The meeting moved slowly and my mind often wandered. I thought of the pressing concerns of the church and I wondered how much longer I could continue to be both a pastor and a professor. They were both full-time jobs, and I seldom had time for my family. Our daughter Damali, now almost a year old, was growing up without me. With this thought my eyes met the eyes of a fellow professor. He was a brilliant man with a compassionate and friendly face, and I saw that he too felt a deep distraction. He looked away, but a few minutes later he spoke aloud. His voice was flat, as if he were living in a dream.

"It is most strange," he said. "Here we are sitting to discuss a five-year plan and just now on my way to this building I passed five dead bodies."

He laughed nervously and looked at the floor. For a few moments no one spoke. When the chairman tried to start the discussion again, there was little response. Our colleague had spoken the secret buried deep in every heart. There was no reason to concern ourselves with five-year plans. It was senseless to talk about the future. It was senseless to talk about tomorrow. I thought of the church elders and our own brave plans to begin a new ministry. What were we thinking? Such plans seemed only idle dreams. We were a whole country of people who from one moment to the next did not know the course of our lives. Only the present was ours.

The meeting was soon closed. Two days later the man who had spoken our deepest fears packed his bags and, without saying good-bye, fled to England.

It was during this time that the first of many public executions were held in Uganda. Early in February Amin arrested 12 Ugandans, including a 16-year-old boy, and accused them of conspiring against the government. The victims were carefully chosen from seven separate townships where Amin needed to solidify his position and each one was executed in his own hometown.

On the day of the executions I drove through Kampala to do some counseling at church. It was late morning and as I approached the downtown area I saw a large crowd streaming towards the Queens Tower, a clock tower not far from the center of town. There was a holiday feeling in the air and it seemed as if almost every man, woman and child in Kampala was on the street. The faces I saw were sometimes bewildered, but most often gay and excited. They were the faces of people whose hopes were defeated but who, for a few hours, would find a scapegoat.

At the bus-park my car was brought to a standstill by a crowd of noisy, gesturing pedestrians. I climbed out of my car to see what was going on. Just at that moment the crowd opened up and I saw a man with a rope around his neck being pulled down the street towards the tower. His hands were tied and sweat streamed down his face. His eyes were wide with terror but he seemed not to notice the shouting and the curses being heaped on his head.

As he passed directly in front of me a young boy to my left clutched the hand of the woman standing next to him and cried out, "Mommy, there goes Daddy!"

I averted my eyes quickly, but at that moment I ceased being a spectator and became one with the man on the rope. *Oh God*, I cried silently, *aren't there enough orphans and widows? Can't you spare the life of this one man?* I watched him stagger down the street until the crowd moved in again and I could no longer see. I returned to my car and took another back road to the church, but by the time I arrived I had lost my strength for counseling. I listened only half-heartedly to the domestic complaints of the couple sitting before me and I soon excused myself and returned home.

The executions were televised all afternoon. In living rooms and bars throughout the city one could witness the killings firsthand. The victims were tied to trees, naked except for the white aprons which enabled the television cameras to show the blood pumping from their chests. Their terror-stricken faces and the shocked expressions of their family and friends stood in sharp contrast to the stony impersonal features of the firing squad. At the last moment the victims were hooded and, to the strains of lively martial music, the command was given to fire. The men slumped forward dead.

The execution tunes played throughout the day, on radios and in the streets. By the end of the day my head was swimming with the sound. And from that day forward, life in Uganda seemed to grow more and more desperate. The church compound was just off the main road between Kampala and Makindye Prison and more than once our services were interrupted by the sounds of inhuman screams coming from passing cars. In the country or in downtown Kampala, it was not unusual to pass a flashy government car and see legs protruding from the trunk.

One day a woman who worked in the food service at Luzira Prison came running to the church vestry during my counseling hours. She was deathly terrified. In a hysterical voice she told me that she had just seen more than 50 human bodies without heads and arms. They had been delivered to the prison in cotton sacks by one of our own church members. The woman demanded that the church take disciplinary action against the man, that we publicly censure him and remove him from our membership rolls. I stared at her, paralyzed with disbelief, and then I shook my head. There was nothing the church could do. If the elders disciplined the man, we would all be killed. If the church censured him, it would be destroyed. There was nothing *anyone* could do. Our helplessness was complete.

The discouragement of these moments gathered like storm clouds over our heads. The order of life we had once known had completely fallen apart, and there were times when it seemed to all of us that God had forgotten our need of Him. But one night in late February, a time when everyone's hopes seemed to have sunk especially low, an elder in the Redeemed Church experienced the special providence of God.

Dr. Joseph K.[12] a leading elder on the church committee, was the distinguished head of one of Kampala's largest hospitals. He had been educated in London, and he and his wife lived in a huge five-bedroom mansion of white brick, with a corrugated iron roof. Their yard was a well-kept garden of exotic plants and Dr. K. was fond of giving tours to his visitors and pointing out the Latin names of all his foliage. He sang in the church choir of the cathedral and was famous for his knowledge of Ugandan traditions and of great Ugandan men of the past.

On this particular night, Dr. K. and his wife had gone to bed early. At midnight their dogs began to bark shrilly and shortly afterwards they heard heavy footsteps on their veranda. The veranda was surrounded by barbed wire and Dr. K. knew immediately that an intruder had come into his yard. He left his bed and took down from the wall a gun which he used in his frequent hunting trips. After loading it, he called his wife and together they sat down in the front room and began praying. Before they finished they heard a noise against their east window and, looking up, they saw the back of a large man. He was leaning heavily against the glass and seemed about to push his way into the room. Dr. K. took his gun into his hands and was preparing to shoot when suddenly his hands began to shake uncontrollably. The doctor was an experienced hunter and had never been intimidated by even the fiercest of animals, but now he found himself unable to pull the trigger.

Just at that moment the front door of their home fell

in. Six Nubians stalked into the parlor. Some were dressed in army uniforms, the rest were wearing brightly-colored flowered shirts. When they saw the doctor with his raised gun, they laughed.

"You are a stupid man," they said. "Give us the gun."

Dr. K. gave it to them and they told him to lie flat on the floor face down. Any movement, they promised, would be his last. Two men remained in the room with him while the others ordered Mrs. K. to take them through the house and show them where the family's most expensive possessions were kept.

The soldiers took whatever they could lay their hands on: money, silver, clothes, dishes, radios and the television. When they finished their plundering, they loaded everything into the doctor's car, including his gun, and drove away cheering and laughing. As they headed down the street the doctor and his wife rushed to their parlor window and looked outside. An army van packed with dozens of soldiers was pulling out of the driveway. Dr. K. and his wife understood immediately the miracle that had taken place in their midst: if the doctor's gun had fired, they both would have been killed. They fell to their knees in thanksgiving to God, praising Him for sparing their lives.

The afternoon after the raid, I went to their home to give them my condolences. Dr. K. himself greeted me at the door. He was a partially bald, middle-aged man and although he seemed somewhat distracted he invited me in with the same warm hospitality that always made me look forward to visiting in his home. His wife was in the front room with several neighbors and Dr. K. had been in the middle of telling his story to this small group of sympathizers. My arrival was all the excuse needed to start the story again from the beginning.

Dr. K. spoke with quiet dignity, and I was surprised

to see how little he seemed to have been affected by the raid. It was this same inner strength that had made him one of the most respected elders on the committee of elders. Together, he and Jolly Joe Kiwanuka provided expert leadership for the affairs of the church. They were the best of friends, but while Kiwanuka tended to be aggressive and flamboyant in all his actions, Dr. K. was most often the one to throw oil on troubled waters. He had a gentle manner and in any dispute he was careful to weigh his words so as not to give offense to anyone. In this way he brought a spirit of peace and reconciliation to our sometimes explosive meetings.

When Dr. K. finished his story and his neighbors had excused themselves, he called his wife and me together for prayer. He spoke to God in a humble and confident manner, asking Him to avenge for the sake of His own righteousness the injustices inflicted upon His people. "Father in heaven," he prayed, "we have lost everything, and we have no other court of appeal. Only you can help us. We throw ourselves on your mercy."

Although I had come to Dr. K.'s home prepared for mourning and depression, I left with a heart full of joy. It was true we had no earthly court of appeal. There were no policemen, soldiers or government officials from whom we could seek help. We had nothing left. We had come so low that only God could help us now. I was confident of His mercy.

Two weeks later on a Sunday morning, Dr. K. burst into the vestry of the church. His face was glowing with joy and he could barely restrain himself from laughing as he told his story. The day before, his car had been found in the middle of the road to Katwe, less than a mile from the church. The drivers of the car had been involved in an accident and when witnesses began to gather, they fled the scene. The registration was in Dr.

K.'s name. He was called and when he arrived to claim his car, he found the possessions that had been taken from his home. The mercenaries who robbed him were apparently without a permanent home and they left everything, including his gun, packed tightly in the trunk. The only thing missing was pocket money.

That afternoon, accompanied by loud thanksgivings from the congregation, Dr. K. testified to God's providence before the entire church. When he finished the story of his recovered possessions, he commanded everyone to take off their shoes. "You are standing in the holy of holies," he said. "God is truly in our midst. And if ever you are under attack, if you need to be saved from murderous savages, you do not need to be afraid. Jesus Christ will stand by you."

Dr. K.'s experience with Amin's soldiers brought a deep and rich conviction to his life. From that day onward he was persuaded of God's protection. When months later his life was once again in grave danger, he refused to leave the country.

"God has rescued me from the soldiers once," he said to a friend who brought him a warning, "and He can do it again. He has shown me of His protection and has given me this responsibility. I must stay in Uganda."

Dr. K.'s deliverance brought a new conviction to my own life as well. That Sunday afternoon as I listened to him speak before the church, the disheartening events of the past weeks seemed to roll from my shoulders. I was reminded again of the vision we had shared with the rest of the elders for making the church a channel of God's blessing. Surely in His concern for Dr. K.'s life and possessions, God had confirmed this ministry. In the chaos of our existence, He had spoken clearly of His own faithfulness and reminded us again of His concern for individuals.

10

Human Sorrow, a Distant Grief?

The public executions in February marked the end of civilian government in Uganda. From that day on, Amin's power was absolute. He dismissed his entire cabinet and replaced civilian ministers with Muslim army men. He disarmed the legal Ugandan army and gave Nubian mercenaries the keys to the armory. He drew up new lists of leaders to be killed and commissioned new squads of assassins. Within a year, most of the men who might have saved Uganda from his regime were dead or in exile.

Not long after the executions I returned downtown to do some family errands with my wife. I took Penina to a tailor shop on Kampala Road and then drove three blocks on an errand of my own. The streets were crowded with late morning shoppers and I drove around for several minutes before I found a parking place.

I had just parked and was stepping from my car to the curb when I heard a tremendous explosion. It was followed by smaller explosions and screams of terror. From the direction of the tailor shop huge billowing clouds of black smoke poured into the sky.

I ran towards the smoke with a deep fear in my heart. Hundreds of other people ran wildly in all directions, pushing at each other and screaming. Some shouted, "The mercenaries have blown up the city!" Others cried, "Today we are all dead!" From every corner of the city bells began to ring.

I reached the edge of Kampala Road and from there I saw the tailor shop. A deep relief filled my heart. The shop was still standing. Several hundred yards down the street a wall of flame was shooting high in the air, and against its light I could see the dark shadows of human figures running back and forth. As I ran to the shop door, loud sirens screamed in the air and subsided. The first fire trucks and rescue workers had arrived at the blaze.

I found Penina in the shop taking shelter with the rest of the customers. We embraced with deep feeling. The tailor also greeted me warmly. He had closed his door at the first explosion. He asked me many questions about the fire but I knew nothing and could not answer him. The tailor was a simple man but well-known throughout Kampala; for many months he had been chief tailor to Amin's wives. In two-weeks' time, mercenaries would knock down his door and drag him away. The tailor would disappear, never to be seen again. His shop would be closed only to be reopened, weeks later, as the property of a Nubian.

But I knew nothing of that now. I thanked the tailor for taking care of my wife and said good-bye. Penina and

I hurried to the car and, after much delay and confusion, we arrived home. Penina told me then that with the first explosion she had praised God. "I thought to myself, He has heard our prayers," she said, "He has ended the world."

It was not until late afternoon that we heard the cause of the explosion. A careless smoker had dropped a cigarette by a leaking gasoline truck. Within seconds the truck had exploded into flames and the fire spread quickly to nearby buildings. Before it was controlled, more than 70 people had been killed or seriously injured. Many of the dead were firemen and rescue workers.

That same evening a woman from the church knocked on our door. Her face was numb and her eyes were red from weeping. When I invited her to come inside she refused.

"Please come with me to Mulago Hospital," she said. "My husband has been burned and he is in need of prayers." Her husband was one of the firemen injured in the morning blaze. A burning wall had collapsed on him, and the rescue workers had been delayed. Now he lay near death.

I said good-bye to Penina and went with the woman. Nothing she had told me prepared me for what I found at the hospital. The fire victims had been taken to a large hall and, even before I stepped through the doorway, I could smell the bitter stench of scorched flesh. Inside the room the smell was so strong I could hardly breathe. The groans of the suffering patients and the screams of their weeping relatives filled the air. Only the most fortunate victims had beds. The rest were lying crowded together on straw floor mats. Their exposed flesh was burnt black or inflamed to an ugly red, and most of them would not live out the night.

The woman led me to the bed of her dying husband. I stood beside him and all I could see was scorched flesh. His body was completely disfigured.

"How do you know this is your husband?" I asked gently.

"I can only feel it," she said. "I can only feel that he is the one."

She knelt and began to pray for God's comfort in his life. I knelt beside her but there was no hope in my heart. Perhaps her husband is already dead, I thought to myself. Perhaps he has left this world and it is only the one who stays behind who still suffers and needs comfort. I prayed for the woman beside me and I prayed with tears of deep pain. I asked God to protect her spirit from the Evil One and to send His Comforter to give her strength for the night to come. When I rose to leave, I promised I would come again.

When I returned the following afternoon the fireman was dead—he died a few hours before sunrise. His wife had crawled into a remote corner of the hall and when I found her she had fallen on her face in silent weeping. There were no words to speak; she was alone with her crushed expectations. Two days ago she had a husband with a steady job, yesterday a man in a coma, today nothing. She was a poor woman from northern Uganda, and she had no relatives in the city. Now there was no one to protect her, no love to preserve her.

I sat with the woman for some time and then I walked away. Her dejected lonely face stayed fresh in my mind. I could see orderlies in the hall removing dead bodies from beds to make room for those still living. I could hear the cries of suffering men and women and smell the stench of their burnt flesh. Something seemed crushed inside me. *I need to find a lonelier place*, I said to myself, *I need to sit and be quiet before God*. I wanted to know

111

if it was my false expectations or if the Word of God had failed me. I wanted to know if God would help me understand the world as He did, to know mankind as He knew mankind.

I left the hospital and walked a few blocks down the street to the Uganda Museum. Behind the museum was a field where I had often walked as a student when I wanted to be alone. It was a peaceful clearing, rolling with grassy hills and sloping gently to a stream below. On its western border stood the beautiful homes of Kampala's most exclusive district. On its northern border, across the valley, was a golf course.

The sun was shining brightly and the sky was a deep blue. A slight breeze rippled a sea of wild elephant grass, and hundreds of wild begonias and fireball lilies covered the fields. Butterflies danced in the shade of the eucalyptus trees. Public workers were slashing grass with their machetes and young couples walked slowly over the hills. Down the valley and across the stream I could see the bright green fields of the golf course. Red flags were blowing in the wind and golfers dressed in colorful shirts strolled leisurely over the greens. It was the same landscape I had seen many times before. As I started down the path that led to the valley below, I felt the peace of the day begin to restore my heart.

I was almost to the stream when I saw the soldiers. They had been hidden from my view by a grove of eucalyptus trees. When I came upon them, they were across the stream but less than 30 yards away. Some of them were dressed in uniforms and several wore flowered shirts. Across their shoulders were rifles. At their feet was a man, dressed in a business suit and lying on the ground. The soldiers were kicking him from every side, and I could hear their heavy boots crunching against his flesh. They laughed and cursed as the man groaned, rolling from side to side. He was barely conscious.

One of the soldiers heard my step and looked across the stream to where I stood. He waved his gun in my direction. I knew it was a warning to go away, but I only stared at him transfixed. His gun seemed to me like a tunnel and the whole world began to spin. The soldier looked at me for a few seconds and then shrugged. He turned back to his companions and to the man lying on the ground. With a loud laugh he kicked the man in the head.

From somewhere deep inside my head I heard a cry. *Oh please, oh please, somebody help! Help this dying man! Public workers come on the run and golfers leave your greens. Young people go quickly, ring for the police! Ring for the police, a man is murdered in broad daylight. Ring for the ambulance, he is not yet dead!*

But no words came from my mouth. The public workers went on mowing and the golfers played on to the next hole. The young people walked quickly in other directions. No one seemed to notice the soldiers, no one dared to look in their direction. The soldiers continued in their work with a casual arrogance. They knew there was no one in the world who would rescue their victim.

I walked up from the valley and back to the museum as if in a dream. My plans for meditation and prayer were forgotten. I did not remember why I had come to these fields or where I had been. The whole world seemed to me dead. The man lying on the ground was no more than a stone. The soldiers were only machines. They were nothing to me and I was nothing to them. I was nothing to myself. I had no more human feeling. I could not feel the depth of evil around me and I could not feel the pain of the man lying on the ground. I could only feel the dreamlike deadness of my own body.

113

In that moment I learned a new truth. I learned that just as there is a boundary beyond which human beings cannot comprehend the glory of God, so there is a boundary beyond which they cannot comprehend the evil in the world. There is a boundary beyond which everything is a senseless chasm. It is here in the nightmare of utter chaos that human feeling dies. It is here, where death and terror seem to have full dominion, that even the deepest of human sorrows becomes but a distant grief.

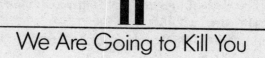

We Are Going to Kill You

Despite the growing shadow of Idi Amin, Easter morning, 1973, began as a most joyous occasion for the Redeemed Church. The sun had just risen and the sky was empty of clouds when the first people began arriving at the compound where we worshiped. They came from almost every tribe, from the Baganda, the Basoga, the Banyankole, the Acholi and the Langi, the Bagweri and the Bagisu. They came from as far away as Masaka, a town 80 miles southwest of Kampala. There were old men with walking sticks and young women with babies on their backs. There were small children with flowers in their arms. There were doctors and lawyers, businessmen and farmers, cotton growers and government workers. Only a few had traveled by private car or taxi. Most came on foot or rode bicycles. Others crowded into lorries so lopsided they seemed ready to collapse at any moment. But however the people traveled, they arrived with the same joyful greeting: *"Aleluya, Azukide!* Hallelujah, He is risen!"

By 9:00 over 7,000 people were gathered. It was the largest crowd ever to attend Sunday service at the Redeemed Church. When there were no more places in the compound, people climbed trees or sat on the roofs of parked lorries. A few large groups set up in nearby yards with their own amplifying systems. Hundreds of others stood in the street.

The compound itself was a most dazzling sight. Church members had come the night before to decorate the surrounding houses and banana trees with bright tropical flowers and crepe-paper streamers. The streamers fluttered in the light morning wind and red-winged birds flew between the trees. On the ground the people sat close together dressed in their finest Sunday garments. The men wore long white robes, *kanzus,* and short black vests. The women were dressed in white or wore the brightly colored *busuti,* a long, native cloth dress with puffed sleeves and a wide sash. The children wore bright dresses or shorts, and their newly-oiled faces shone in the sun.

Before the service, the elders and I met in the "vestry," an empty house by the compound, to pray. We felt deeply the hunger in the hearts of the people who had gathered for worship. We knew their desire to hear the Word of God and we prayed that their lives would be transformed by its power. As we poured our hearts out to the Father in agonizing intercession, desperate scenes from the previous weeks flashed again in my mind. I saw a face burned beyond recognition, and a woman huddled in a corner weeping. I saw a crowd of soldiers standing in the park cheering, and heard the sound of boot crunching against bone. I remembered the arrogance of the mercenaries, and the dreamlike deadness of my heart. Once again the triumph of evil overwhelmed me. I felt a deep fear. I myself had fallen, how could I hope to strengthen others? Who was I to feed God's children in this most desperate hour? What words could I speak? My brothers and sisters needed courage to stand firm in the growing terror. They needed strength to sustain them in suffering. They did not need my sermon. They did not need my thoughts on the Resurrection. My father had been right. "In such times men do not need words," he had said. "They need power."

As I prayed for strength and wisdom, the words of Matthew 14:19 came to my mind. It was the same text that a brother from the Revival Fellowship had read to me many years before.

> *And taking the five loaves and the two fish he looked up to heaven, and blessed, and broke and gave the loaves to the disciples, and the disciples gave them to the crowds.*

With this verse, I heard the convicting voice of the Holy Spirit. It was Jesus who provided bread for the crowds. The disciples' task was only to distribute what their Master had already given them. It was God who sustained His people. He was not asking me to feed His children from the words of my own heart. He was only asking me to distribute the living bread He had put into my hand.

I took my Bible and went to preach that Easter morning with new courage. My message was the suffering of Jesus Christ. I spoke of His triumph over evil and His victory over death. I spoke of the power of His resurrection. Behind me were the elders, sitting on a bench and praying. In front of me were thousands of unfamiliar faces. There were believers in need of encouragement and unbelievers in need of salvation. There were widows

117

and orphans. There was an informer with his cassette. Perhaps there were members of the State Research Bureau. But Christ, the Living Bread of the world was there, and that made the difference.

At 12:30 the sun was pouring hot on our heads and I tried to close the service. The people refused to leave. "We have not come for a church service," someone shouted. "We have come to hear the Word of God! Go rest yourself and come back to preach again!" The crowd clapped and shouted their approval. I went to the vestry for a brief rest and returned in the mid-afternoon. Hardly a person had moved. I preached for three more hours and this time when I finished, no one objected. The sun was going down and everyone knew the hour had come to close the meeting. It was not safe to travel after dark.

I closed the service with the benediction. In the uncertainty of our lives and with the nearness of death, the words of Simeon held deep meaning:

> *Lord, now lettest thou thy servant depart in peace, according to thy word; for mine eyes have seen thy salvation, which thou hast prepared before the face of all people.* [13]

We did not know when we would see each other again or when God might call us home. But we went out in peace because we had seen with our eyes the salvation of the Lord.

With a loud amen from the people and a final chorus from the choir the Easter service ended. I turned to the elders and we embraced, praising God. It seemed as if days instead of hours had passed since we had met for prayer. I was exhausted, but there was joy in my heart. God had answered our prayers: He had broken bread and fed His people.

I greeted several more friends and then left for the vestry to change my clothes, hoping to have a few minutes alone in prayer. I had to push my way through the crowd and when I finally arrived at the house I was exhausted. I was too tired to notice the men behind me until they had closed the door.

There were five of them. They stood between me and the door, pointing their rifles at my face. Their own faces were scarred with the distinctive tribal cuttings of the Kakwa tribe. They were dressed casually in flowered shirts and bell-bottom pants, and wore sunglasses. Although I had never seen any of them before, I recognized them immediately. They were the secret police of the State Research Bureau—Amin's Nubian assassins.

For a long moment no one said anything. Then the tallest man, obviously the leader, spoke. "We are going to kill you," he said. "If you have something to say, say it before you die." He spoke quietly but his face was twisted with hatred.

I could only stare at him. For a sickening moment I felt the full weight of his rage. We had never met before but his deepest desire was to tear me to pieces. My mouth felt heavy and my limbs began to shake. Everything left my control. *They will not need to kill me*, I thought to myself. *I am just going to fall over. I am going to fall over dead and I will never see my family again.* I thought of Penina home alone with Damali. What would happen to them when I was gone?

From far away I heard a voice, and I was astonished to realize that it was my own. "I do not need to plead my own cause," I heard myself saying. "I am a dead man already. My life is dead and hidden in Christ. It is your lives that are in danger, you are dead in your sins. I will pray to God that after you have killed me, He will spare you from eternal destruction."

119

The tall one took a step towards me and then stopped. In an instant, his face was changed. His hatred had turned to curiosity. He lowered his gun and motioned to the others to do the same. They stared at him in amazement but they took their guns from my face.

Then the tall one spoke again. "Will you pray for us now?" he asked.

I thought my ears were playing a trick. I looked at him and then at the others. My mind was completely paralyzed. The tall one repeated his question more loudly, and I could see that he was becoming impatient.

"Yes, I will pray for you," I answered. My voice sounded bolder even to myself. "I will pray to the Father in heaven. Please bow your heads and close your eyes."

The tall one motioned to the others again, and together the five of them lowered their heads. I bowed my own head, but I kept my eyes open. The Nubian's request seemed to me a strange trick. Any minute, I thought to myself, my life will end. I did not want to die with my eyes closed.

"Father in heaven," I prayed, "you who have forgiven men in the past, forgive these men also. Do not let them perish in their sins but bring them into yourself."

It was a simple prayer, prayed in deep fear. But God looked beyond my fears and when I lifted my head, the men standing in front of me were not the same men who had followed me into the vestry. Something had changed in their faces.

It was the tall one who spoke first. His voice was bold but there was no contempt in his words. "You have helped us," he said, "and we will help you. We will speak to the rest of our company and they will leave you alone. Do not fear for your life. It is in our hands and you will be protected."

I was too astonished to reply. The tall one only motioned for the others to leave. He himself stepped to the doorway and then he turned to speak one last time. "I saw widows and orphans in your congregation," he said. "I saw them singing and giving praise. Why are they happy when death is so near?"

It was still difficult to speak but I answered him. "Because they are loved by God. He has given them life, and will give life to those they loved, because they died in Him."

His question seemed strange to me, but he did not stay to explain. He only shook his head in perplexity and walked out the door.

I stared at the open door of the vestry for several moments and then sat down on a nearby straw mat chair. My knees were no longer strong and I could feel my whole body tremble. I could not think clearly. Less than 10 minutes before, I had considered myself a dead man. Even though I was surrounded by 7,000 people there was no human being to whom I could appeal. I could not ask Kiwanuka to use his connections, I could not ask the elders to pray, I could not appeal to the mercy of the Nubian killers. My mouth had frozen and I had no clever words to speak. In that moment, with death so near, it was not my sermon that gave me courage, or an idea from Scripture. It was Jesus Christ, the living Lord.

I drove home that Easter evening deeply puzzled but with joy in my heart. I felt that I had passed from death to life, and that I could now speak in one mind with Paul:

> *I have been crucified with Christ and I no longer live, but Christ lives in me. The life I live in the body, I live by faith in the Son of God, who loved me and gave himself for me.* [14]

12
I Hear Their Screams

The days that followed my Easter brush with death were days for sober thinking. I did not see the Nubians again and the initial excitement I had felt over the sudden change in their intentions was replaced almost overnight by a deep suspicion. Their behavior had been mysterious, to say the least, and I wondered if what I thought to be God's providence was only a masquerade. Perhaps the men would now fake conversions to infiltrate the church. I had heard that this was common practice in Communist countries and it was well known that Amin was receiving strategy lessons from the Russians. Or perhaps the Nubians had a more private agenda. Maybe they were only waiting for a spectacular, public moment in which to do their killing.

With these thoughts heavy on our minds, Penina and I spent long hours together discussing the possibility of my resigning from active participation in the church ministry. There were more reasons than the Nubians for taking such a step. Conditions in Uganda seemed to be worsening daily. Amin was now publicly chanting praises to Adolf Hitler, claiming that Hitler had not gone far enough in burning only six million Jews. In November he had arrested and executed a fellow evangelist for reading a passage of Scripture from Isaiah which spoke of the Israelites' ultimate victory over their enemies. At the same time, Amin's soldiers were becoming more and more aggressive in their attacks. It had become dangerous even for ordinary citizens to drive their cars at night. Gangs of drunken Nubians patrolled the roads and often stopped drivers, beat them badly, took their cars, and left them lying in ditches.

Most frightening of all, an increasing number of Ugandans were turning against their fellow villagers and townsmen. Personal grudges which in times past had been forgotten or settled privately were now occasions for bloodshed. It was easy to bribe army officers to arrest or kill one's enemies, and there was never any danger for the offended party.

Even in the church there was no safety. I had learned in the past month that one of our most active members, a man on the committee of elders, was informing on our congregation for the government. He was a quiet, shrewd man, tall and well-built, and extremely skilled in working with his hands. Whenever there was a church project requiring manual skills, he was always the first to volunteer. I had never known him well but when I heard of his spying activities in our congregation I was deeply hurt. I went to Katongole Sabaganzi for advice and after I finished pouring out my frustration and disappointment, the wise man whose strong words had begun the Redeemed Church only shook his head. It seemed to me then that in the past two years he had aged a great deal. He, like Kiwanuka, had spent himself for the cause of Uganda's freedom and now something in his bearing spelled disappointment and defeat. While he was careful not to show his fears, I saw that a shadow of concern crossed his face. After a moment of silence he finally said, in his sad, wise way, "Kefa, there is nothing you can do. There is no community on earth where there is not a Judas."

In these conditions, where survival was difficult for everyone, it seemed foolish for me to add to my own danger and the danger to my family by remaining at the head of the Redeemed Church. I had no formal or financial connection with the church and many of the elders were equally qualified for preaching responsibilities. Furthermore, in the last months I had spent less and less time at Makerere University and there were numerous things I now needed to do in order to finish out the year. In six weeks' time Penina and I would be leaving Uganda for several months of study in Holland. Through the efforts of Dr. Hans Rookmaaker I had recently been awarded a graduate fellowship at the Free University of Amsterdam, and as soon as the school year ended at Makerere University, Penina and I were going to fly to Amsterdam. Perhaps by the time I had finished my doctoral candidacy exams, the political situation in Uganda would have stabilized. Or perhaps at least whoever it was that wanted me killed would have forgotten the whole affair.

Penina and I had all but decided that I should leave the ministry when the tall Nubian I had encountered on Easter morning paid his second visit to the church vestry. I had just finished counseling with a young woman whose husband had been murdered by mercenaries when the man walked through the door. I recognized him immediately, and the same fear I had felt while looking down the barrel of his gun gripped me again. I thought I was going to be killed.

The Nubian nodded a greeting and spoke with the same abruptness as before. "Now that I am a *balokole*, a born again one," he asked, "what do I do next?"

It seemed to me then that there would be no end to the surprises I would receive in my life. But I tried to hide my amazement and I answered the man in the same straightforward manner with which he himself had spoken. If he was claiming for himself a new life in Christ then, at least for the time being, I could only take him at his word.

"You need to find a Bible," I said. "I cannot tell you what to do, only Jesus Christ can. You need to read His message and see for yourself."

I told him, as I told all new converts, to begin by reading the Gospel of John. The Nubian nodded his assent, and left. Four days later, he was back again. As soon as he walked through the door I could see that he was deeply disturbed. His muscles twitched and he clenched and unclenched his hands as if he could barely keep himself from springing on someone.

"Read this," he said, without any greeting at all. He shoved a Swahili Bible into my hands and pointed to John 8:44. I read aloud;

> *You belong to your father, the devil and you want to carry out your father's desire. He was a murderer from the beginning not holding to the truth for there is no truth in him. When he lies, he speaks his native language, for he is a liar and the father of lies.*

The Nubian looked at me expectantly but I waited for him to speak.

"Don't you see," he said, his voice trembling. "Jesus is talking about me. I have killed over 200 people. I murdered them with my own hands. Nothing stopped me. I never showed mercy. And all the time I thought I was working for Amin but I have been working for Satan. It is he who is my father!"

I remained silent and the man sat down on a nearby chair, weeping. After several moments he became quiet and then in a broken voice he told me his story.

"All my life," he said, "I have been dominated by hatred. My stepfather never cared for me, I was always beaten. He beat my mother too and when I saw her lying crushed on the floor I was sick to my stomach. But she never loved me. She hated me and treated me as a burden. By the time I was a man, I had so much hatred. I never knew love. I started killing people and at first it was hard. But once you kill one person you can go on forever. There is so much guilt, you cannot stop. You cannot admit that you hate yourself, and that you have done this terrible thing."

The Nubian spoke so intensely that sweat began dripping from his face. *I am looking at a man who has come to his end*, I thought to myself. *He has no more mental or emotional strength.*

The Nubian continued with his story.

"When we came to kill you Easter morning," he said, "we were going to kill you in front of everyone. We were going to show you our power. But we kept sitting in the service. I didn't hear anything you said, I could only see the widows and orphans who were sitting around me. Some of them I knew. I had killed their men with my own hands, and I expected them to be weeping and mourning. But they were clapping, they were singing songs and they were happy. Their joy made me so afraid. I thought to myself, if for one moment I could understand it, I would give up everything.

"When we came to this room and you prayed for us, I did understand. I felt something in my life I had never felt before. But now I have read of this man Jesus. And I cannot believe. I cannot be forgiven. My father is Satan. Every night I go to bed and see the faces of the people I have killed. I hear their screams and the screams of their women and children. I never heard them before, but now I hear nothing else. They never leave my heart and I cannot be forgiven."

As I listened to him pour out his torment, my fear for my own life completely disappeared. I wanted to comfort him, to convince him of God's forgiveness but I could find no words to speak. For a moment I myself even doubted that God would want to forgive such a man. How much human misery he had brought to our lives! How many people he had destroyed! I thought of the Okelo family and their bloodstained living room. Perhaps this man had been the one who tortured and tore them limb from limb.

With a great effort I pushed these thoughts aside and picked up my Bible. In the past months my own speech had often failed me but the words of Scripture had been life and truth. Now I read with the Nubian testimony after testimony of God's love and forgiveness. When we had finished, the words of Isaiah had become a new and living reality for us both:

> *I have blotted out, as a thick cloud, thy trans-gressions, and, as a cloud, thy sins: return unto me; for I have redeemed thee.* [15]

The Nubian prayed that God would continue to reveal to him the truth of His Word and together we asked God to empower us by the Holy Spirit, that we might believe in the forgiveness of sins.

On the following Sunday I saw the Nubian again. He and the four men who had invaded the church vestry were now attending our church services and afterwards he came alone to meet me in the vestry. His face was covered with a broad smile and he moved as if he were about to dance.

"I have found the love of Jesus Christ," he said. "I am a new man. I can feel it, my sins have been taken away. A few days ago I was ordered on a raiding mission by my commander. When we came to the house we were supposed to plunder, I pointed my gun in the face of the owner and he was trembling. Then I told him, 'You are a lucky man. If I had met you two weeks ago you would be a dead man. But I have met Jesus Christ and my sins have been forgiven. I am a free man and I will free you.' Then I let him go."

I was so happy to see the transformation in the Nubian's life that I hardly noticed his strange method of evangelism. Later, when it came to mind, I did not know whether to laugh or to sigh. Testifying from behind a loaded gun! The chaos of Amin's regime was certainly producing bizarre testimonies.

From this man I learned anew that the blood of Jesus Christ covers a multitude of sins. The Nubian was a man whose life had been shaped by the absence of God's love. From the beginning he had been a rejected personality, a man who hated his own image. He had tried to recapture his human dignity by destroying other human beings, but he had only fallen deeper into self-hatred and insecurity. It was a vicious circle: the more he hated himself the more cruelly he acted, and the more cruelly he acted the more he hated himself. But now, by the love of Jesus Christ, he had been released from this bondage. He had a new and secure identity as a child of God.

I thought of Idi Amin. His father had left him at birth and his mother had toured army barracks as a camp prostitute. His tribe, the Sudanese Nubians, had become notorious for their sadistic brutality and vengeful spirits.

Perhaps Amin too was a man who had never known God's love. Perhaps he too found his self-worth only in hating. If so, his insecurity could only become paranoia. Hundreds of thousands of people had died by his hand and at the hands of his Nubian mercenaries. In a society of extended families, where one death means two hundred enemies, such crimes were unforgivable. Amin's enemies were innumerable, and the more he tried to eliminate them, the more new enemies he made. He too was caught in a vicious cycle. He would never be able to stop killing. He would never be able to make himself secure.

The Nubian's testimony gave me the courage I needed to remain in the church ministry. My concern for my own safety became secondary to my desire to witness the power of God, and I knew that as a community of believers we of the Redeemed Church were experiencing His grace now more than ever before. We were learning to live in the everlasting now, to let Scripture alone form our expectations and to pray without complaining. It was no longer the days themselves that we desired, but the forgiveness and the love of God. In the uncertainty of our day-to-day existence, we were being delivered from our reliance on methods, from the idols of self-trust and self-pity. We could no longer afford to ask converts, "Do you believe?" We asked, "Are you ready to die for Jesus Christ?"

My lingering doubts about being involved with the church were erased one Sunday morning when Katongole spoke to the congregation. He stood up just as the service was about to begin and immediately a deep hush fell over the compound. By that time our church attendance had swollen to over 14,000 people, but Katongole had an orator's voice and seemingly without effort he made himself heard throughout the compound.

"Many of us do not have long to live," he said, "and we need to hear the words of our Lord." He read from Revelation 11 and stopped at verse 7:

And when they shall have finished their testimony, the beast that ascendeth out of the bottomless pit shall make war against them, and shall overcome them, and kill them.

"By these words we are comforted," Katongole continued. He stood tall in the dignity of his age and position, and I could no longer see any trace of defeat in his bearing. "God has called us for a mission and we are prisoners to His gospel. We live only by His predetermined counsel and we do not need to worry about dying. We will not see death until we have finished our testimony. We are comforted but we are challenged. We are challenged by the believers who have gone before us in the fight against Satan:

'*They overcame him by the blood of the Lamb, and by the word of their testimony; they did not love their lives so much as to shrink from death.*'[16]

Brothers and sisters, we must not love our lives too much, and we must not shrink from death. The message we carry is a greater treasure than our earthly existence. We must be ready to die for the testimony of Jesus Christ."

When Katongole finished speaking there was a long silence throughout the congregation. From my seat on the podium I looked out over the compound at the hushed crowd and saw a sea of somber, expectant faces. The people were waiting, that much I knew. But whether they were waiting for the present storm to pass or for a future storm to come, I could not tell.

Return to Amsterdam

In late April I taught my last class at Makerere University. Three days later, at the end of months of delay in obtaining our air ticket, Penina and I flew with our daughter Damali to Amsterdam. By 1973 the government of Uganda was exercising strict control over the economy, and to stop the flow of shillings from the country they actively discouraged Ugandans from traveling abroad. In order to purchase our airline tickets I had to involve myself in a bureaucratic maze which extended from the Bank of Uganda to the Minister of Finance. Even then, it is unlikely that I would have received my tickets had it not been for the generous efforts of a former schoolmate, a clerk in the Bank of Uganda.

Contrary to my worst expectations, the weeks since Katongole had delivered his somber exhortation had been a time of renewal and growth for the congregation of the Redeemed Church. Through the evangelistic efforts of our members hundreds of new convert were won to Christ and our membership rolls almost doubled. Kiwanuka had secured the complete confidence of the church committee and was providing strong spiritual leadership in matters of church policy and discipleship. He had used his still considerable influence with Amin and other government officials to rescue several church members from prison and he was confident that no further trouble would come to the church from the president's office.

At the same time, all five of the Nubians who had invaded my vestry on Easter morning were now claiming a new commitment to Jesus Christ. They used their privileged access to army information to warn church members whose lives were in danger, and assisted several families in their escape across the Uganda-Kenya border. Their good works were much praised but I remained suspicious of their intentions and never trusted myself to them. I was certain that if the church came in direct conflict with the government, the Nubians would reassert their allegiance to Amin and assist in our destruction.

Despite these hidden fears which I carried with me from Uganda, our return to Amsterdam was a most joyous occasion. From the first, Penina and I had loved the city's European atmosphere, its canals, the buzzing of the trams in the narrow cobbled streets, the speeding motorists careening around sharp irregular corners, and the thousands of cyclists who casually ignored the commotion around them. Every morning from 10:00 to 11:00 we would see the housewives of Amsterdam shaking their dust brooms from gabled attic windows. After hours of polishing they opened their doors to display their handiwork, and sat down to tea. The husband's role, it was clear, was to discuss and debate. On the television, on the radio, and in the home, there seemed no topic too obscure or distinction too subtle for Dutch men. They approached every issue with smoking pipes and passionate gestures and, occasionally, energetic shouts.

Penina and I loved this intellectual intensity of the Dutch but we were touched most personally by their open hearted generosity. In 1970, when we first came to Amsterdam for my studies at the Free University, we were warmly received and soon made many lasting friendships. In that same year Penina became ill with an undiagnosed muscular disorder. She spent months in a wheelchair, paralyzed from her waist down, and while the doctors disagreed on the cause, they were unanimous on the effect: Penina would never walk again.

During this time our medical bills were enormous and the Free University spent far beyond our allotted scholarship funds. One day, when the future seemed to us most dark, I went to the head of the foreign student department, Mr. Baas, and thanked him for his help. I was on the verge of tears and found it difficult to speak. When I mentioned repayment of our debt, Mr. Baas shook his head. He stood up from his chair and putting his hand on my shoulder he spoke words which have never left my memory.

"Kefa," he said, "there is nothing you can repay. Perhaps you are thinking now that giving is a two-way street but to tell the truth it is a flowing river. It does not stop or return but only passes on. Someday soon Penina will be well and you will have your own opportunity. But it will not be an opportunity to repay those from whom you have received, it will be a time to pass your gifts on to someone else."

Mr. Baas had been right. In the weeks to come Penina stubbornly refused to stay in bed. Before long, she was walking. Now, on our second visit to Amsterdam, she was almost completely recovered. Her restored health made our reunion with old friends a time full of thanksgivings.

We were especially glad for our time with Dr. and Mrs. Rookmaaker. We spent long hours with Mrs. Rookmaaker discussing the progress of the orphanage and she had many practical ideas for its future development. Anky Rookmaaker, with her brown curly hair and gentle presence was an attractive, strong-minded woman. She combined her compassion for the poor and homeless with a wise practicality and unsentimental view of suffering. Once when she requested pictures of orphaned children to be used for soliciting Dutch sponsors, I sent her photographs of the children taken in their miserable living conditions. Mrs. Rookmaaker returned the pictures with a sharp rebuke.

"These pictures are ugly," she wrote. "Please send me new pictures when the children have eaten properly for several weeks and are dressed in mended clothes. We don't want to appeal to human sorrow or pity, we want to appeal to what is best in our sponsors. We want to remind them that these children in need are God's handiwork, that they are His beautiful creation."

Mrs. Rookmaaker's views were never conventional, and everything I had come to expect from relief work, she denied. She carried out her own alternatives and in the process gave dignity and respect to hundreds of orphans whom she had never seen, but loved as gifts from God.

Working with Dr. Rookmaaker was equally challenging. Hans Rookmaaker was a middle-aged, stocky man with graying hair who never went anywhere without his pipe. During World War II he had been active in the Dutch Resistance and after being captured by the Germans he was sent to a Nazi concentration camp. There he began to read the Bible. Like Joseph Kiwanuka he found himself strongly drawn to Jesus Christ, the Man of freedom, and after much reflection, he committed his life to his Redeemer. When the war ended, he was released from prison and immediately joined a church. He was surprised to find that church people, of all people, were still in bondage to their sins. Having been himself freed from both physical and spiritual chains, he began a one-man crusade for Christian freedom. Wherever he spoke, he urged people to confess their sins and accept their forgiveness in Christ.

"You are free," he often reminded his Christian brothers and sisters. "Don't forge new chains for yourselves out of false guilt. Christ has not come to make you a pale gray model of mediocrity; He has come to free you to be truly human, to be a passionate, thoughtful, colorful child of God."

As a Christian scholar Dr. Rookmaaker had a profound influence. He established Christian arts groups throughout Europe and urged Christians in the arts not to make a false division between their vocation and their faith. His interest in contemporary culture and his concern for young people led him to found the Eck en Wiel study center, a housing community outside Amsterdam where dozens of students came to spend their summers. These students brought with them philosophical and religious questions as well as pressing personal problems, and at Eck en Wiel they found not only a stimulating intellectual environment but a warm Christian community. Many who arrived with cynical suspicion left with restored minds and a new relationship to Jesus Christ.

As an art historian Dr. Rookmaaker was most provocative and my summer of study with him passed quickly. My only disappointment was found in the school library where I scanned daily the international newspapers. No mention was ever made of the slaughter in Uganda. The sounds of widows and orphans which were heard so clearly in the confines of our small country were not heard at all by the rest of the world. When Idi Amin was mentioned, it was as an international buffoon whose strange exploits bemused the civilized world. The United States ambassador to Uganda, Dr. Thomas Melady, tried to convince his government to make an international issue of Amin's genocide, but the American embassy was soon to close without fanfare, and only on the grounds of a potential security threat to American citizens.

Most disturbing to me was the response from our own continent. The tenth anniversary celebration of the Organization for African Unity (OAU) was held in early August and Amin was received with cheers and laughter. Black Africans saw him only as a brave man who stood up to white imperialists; they could not see him as a genocidal tyrant. Only Presidents Julius Nyerere of Tanzania and Kenneth Kaunda of Zambia opposed his regime.

Without support from the western world and with the people of Africa closing their eyes to our suffering, there seemed to me little hope for rescue. Our own legal army had been without weapons and leadership for two years, and *coups* attempted from within the ranks only served to cement Amin's power. Even his strongest opponents came to suspect that Amin's claims for himself were true: he was invincible, no one could harm him.

In July we received a letter from Adoniya Kirinda, an elder in the Redeemed Church who had taken on temporary responsibility for the Kijomanyi Children's Home. He mentioned briefly a problem of bicycles for the children and then ended his note with a cryptic line:

> *News has just come over the radio calling religious leaders of the Redeemed Church to report to the office of the President. By the time this letter reaches you, the meetings will be completed.*

Kirinda's letter was the last letter we received that was not stamped by the censor in the office of the president and from then on we received no substantial news from home. Mrs. Rookmaaker was deeply disturbed by this turn of events and advised us to remain in Holland until the political situation in Uganda had stabilized. On her suggestion I applied for an extended leave from Makerere University and my application was accepted almost immediately. The Free University once again extended themselves to the physical and financial needs of my family, and my doctoral exams were postponed until early September.

By late August both Penina and I were anxious to return to Uganda and we arranged our return flight for the morning after my exam. To our disappointment, and with only a week to go, the examining board delayed its meeting for three days and we were forced to reschedule our flight. We wired home our change in plans and two days later we received a telegram from Kampala. It was unsigned and the message was short: *travel undercover.*

We showed the telegram to Mrs. Rookmaaker and she again asked us to remain in Amsterdam. This time both Penina and I thought it best to return home. We had been gone for over four months and the ministry of the church was heavy on our minds. We did not want to be separated from our people any longer, and if difficulties arose for us, we were quite certain that Kiwanuka would be able to handle them.

On the morning of my exam, we received two more telegrams. One was unsigned and simply read: *wait*. The other was from Dr. K. and he too advised us to return undercover. By this time, Penina and I were both quite perplexed but we were still agreed in our strong determination to carry through with our plans.

That afternoon I sat for my exam, and passed. In the evening we attended a festive farewell party where we said good-bye to our friends and officials from the university. Mrs. Rookmaaker made one last attempt to persuade us to remain and then, with genuine anxiety, she handed us two "safety" airline tickets. The tickets were for a return flight from Kampala to Amsterdam and had been purchased for us, at Mrs. Rookmaaker's request, by a joint agreement between the university's foreign student department and the Stitching: Save a Child organization. Penina and I were deeply touched by their gift and, after thanking Mrs. Rookmaaker, we resolved to use the tickets upon our return for sending two more students from Uganda to the study center at Eck en Wiel.

Looking backwards from our present position of security, it is difficult to understand how we failed to hear the voice of God in Mrs. Rookmaaker's concern and in the messages from our friends. But, for reasons God Himself only knows, our ears were deafened. On the following morning, Monday, September 16, we boarded a plane for Kampala.

14

We No Longer Follow Kefa

We arrived at Entebbe Airport at 6:00 in the evening, 12 hours after leaving Amsterdam. Despite a delay in Rome and our eager anticipation to be home, the time in the air passed quickly. Penina and I were in high spirits and as we played and laughed with Damali, we talked together of the future. Penina was expecting our second child and I would soon be busy with school and church work, but before long we hoped to begin a study center like the one we had visited in Eck en Wiel. We had met many students there in the summer who had been healed of bitterness they held against their parents and their country, and even themselves. If such was the power of Christian community in an affluent society, what might be accomplished in our country, where 90 percent of the people now lived in dehumanizing misery and terror? Penina and I were convinced that once Amin was gone, a study center could serve to bring healing and reconciliation to Uganda's young.

We stepped from the plane just as the sun was setting over the airport. In the distance I could see scattered clouds colored in a rich violet red and beside me I heard Penina take a long deep breath. I knew that we both felt the same; we were glad to be home.

The airport was far less crowded than usual and its empty corridors seemed almost solemn in their tranquility. We passed through customs quickly. As I picked up our suitcases and stepped around the counter, I saw in front of me Ali S., [17] one of the five Nubians who had come to the church vestry on Easter morning. Ali was a muscular, athletic man who carried himself as a trained soldier in every situation. I remembered well the week before our departure to Holland when Ali had brought his wife to the vestry of the Redeemed Church. For years the woman had been hearing voices and she often woke up in the middle of the night screaming, having dreamed of being strangled in her sleep. Ali visited every witch doctor in Kampala but none were powerful enough to effect a cure. It was then that he came to the church vestry, wanting to know if Jesus could save his wife. The elders and I anointed her with oil, and prayed for her before the service. When next we saw Ali he was beaming with joy. He told us with deep pleasure that his wife no longer had nightmares, and no longer heard strange voices.

Now, seeing that Ali had come to meet us I felt a pleasure of my own. I walked towards him smiling a greeting but as we came together I saw that his face was a stern mask. He looked once over his shoulder and, without ceremony, he grabbed my arm and propelled me towards the door.

"Your arrival here is highly private," he said, speaking quickly in a low voice. "If not for God's care, you are a dead man. There is a blue car waiting for you outside under the lamp post. Go to it now and the driver will take care of you."

I stared at Ali without comprehension.

"Go!" he whispered fiercely.

He shoved me towards the door and pushed Penina, who was carrying Damali, after me. Without thinking, we walked outside. Under the lamp post was a dark blue car with its motor running. Penina and I hurried towards it and as we did, a man whom we didn't know jumped from the front seat and opened the back door. He motioned for us to get in and I felt a stab of fear. *It's a trap. I'm leading my family to their death.* A dozen anxious thoughts crowded into my mind. And then, before I ever understood what was happening, I was inside the car and Penina and Damali were sitting beside me.

The driver turned immediately to greet us and I felt my muscles go weak with relief. It was Elijah O., a close friend, who with his wife had taken care of our house for the summer. Elijah was an auto mechanic and a tall, openhearted member of our own Baganda tribe. His welcome was warm, but brief, and he drove from the airport quickly and without explanation. As soon as possible, he turned off Entebbe Road and headed for Kampala by a long circuitous route. He drove with intense concentration and whenever lights appeared in the road ahead, he changed directions or pulled the car off the road.

For what seemed like an eternity of silence no one spoke. The only sound was the crackling of Elijah's shortwave radio as it monitored nearby police reports. Finally, after more than 30 minutes of suspense and bewilderment, Elijah turned to us and introduced the man beside him as a friend of Ali's. Then he explained our situation.

"Kefa," he said, looking at me anxiously from his rear-view mirror, "you are a marked man. The news of your homecoming spread too far and hundreds of people went to the airport on Friday to welcome you home. There was to be a joyful greeting and Kiwanuka even hired buses! But then you didn't come. So there was a great commotion and before the night was over, Amin himself was on the alert."

Headlights appeared up ahead of us on the road and the night seemed suddenly ominous. Elijah turned quickly off onto a dirt road and it was a long time before he began speaking again. When he did, the story was chilling.

The telegram announcing our new arrival time had not reached Uganda until Saturday, too late to prevent our friends and church members from making a trip to Entebbe Airport. Their excitement and large numbers had been reported immediately to Amin. That night as the Redeemed Church prepared for its Friday prayer service a member of the congregation caught sight of Hussein Malire, the Nubian head of Makindye Prison, driving on the side road next to the church compound.[18] Malire, easily recognizable by his enormous size and the jagged tribal scars running from his forehead to his jaw, was Amin's most notorious killer. He and Kiwanuka had known each other for years, and it was to Malire that Kiwanuka went when he needed to use his influence to rescue men from prison or execution. Makindye Prison itself was less than a mile from the church, and after some discussion, Kiwanuka and the elders dismissed Malire's presence at the church compound as a matter of personal curiosity.

Midway through the service, armed soldiers burst

into the compound. They fired their rifles into the air and in the silence which followed their leader demanded to know who was in charge of the church. Many of the elders, not including Kiwanuka, were arrested on the spot and dragged away in front of the congregation. They were thrown into army vans and in spite of Kiwanuka's efforts to free them they were taken to Makindye Prison. There, in a savage interrogation which lasted throughout the night, they were beaten until many vomited blood. The following morning they were released on condition that they find the preacher Sempangi and turn him over to the police.

That afternoon the telegram announcing our new arrival time came through from Amsterdam. It was channeled immediately to the censorship committee, and then passed on to the president's office. But before the telegram could reach Amin it was intercepted by a friend of Ali's who held an important government position. The official turned the telegram over to Ali, and Ali immediately burned it. He told only Elijah of our new arrival date.

When Elijah finished his story, he did not speak again. I felt the night outside invading our automobile, and it crushed down inside me. That the elders should be beaten and tortured on my account was more than I could bear. *Now they regret everything*, I told myself. *I led them to Christ and promoted them to positions of spiritual leadership and it has come to nothing. Their deaths will be on my head.* The knowledge that I myself might soon die as well came to me with some satisfaction. But it did not remove my sense of guilt; I was trapped within the darkness of my heart.

We drove through the outskirts of Kampala towards the city lights and suddenly I realized we were driving past Makindye Prison and the church compound. I did not want to see either place ever again. I turned my face away from the window and, as if in a dream, I heard the Queens Tower strike the time. It was 8:30. We had been on the road for an hour and a half. An hour and a half, when Entebbe Airport was 21 miles from Kampala. I wondered where we were going, and if we would get there. And suddenly I realized that, during the entire trip, I had not spoken a single word to Penina.

I turned to her and in the darkness I could see only the outline of her face and the sleeping form of Damali in her arms. But I knew that she, like myself, was afraid. I took her hand in my own and my self-pity disappeared.

"We are soon home," I said softly. Penina squeezed my hand and although it was dark, I knew that she smiled. For a time, we were both comforted.

At that same moment, only a few miles away, Elijah's wife Maria opened the door of our home to a knock which she thought to be her husband's. Instead of Elijah, she saw a huge man in military dress with jagged scars running down his face. The man grabbed her wrist and demanded to know where I was. Maria had no idea and was mute with astonishment and terror. Outside on the lawn she saw the headlights of army vans. Soldiers were prowling around the yard with their rifles and in a sudden flash of recognition, Maria realized that the man holding her arm was Hussein Malire. She opened her mouth to scream and fainted dead away. When she awoke sometime later, the door was open and she was alone in the house.

Driving with Elijah, we knew nothing of Maria's danger. We passed by Makerere University, once the proud center of learning for the whole of East Africa, and both Penina and I were struck by its eerie silence.

"Last week," Elijah said, speaking suddenly, "the president of the Makerere student body publicly de-

nounced Amin and demanded his resignation. The boy
was arrested right away, and his professors charged with
brainwashing the young. Except for two of them, who
were shot outright, they have all been thrown into
Makindye Prison."

I was about to ask the professors' names when Elijah
made an abrupt turn off the main road. He drove behind
a dwelling which stood in complete darkness and then
stopped the car, motioning silently for us to get out. It
was not until we were safely inside that he spoke again.

"This house was abandoned by Americans," he said.
"They left all their furniture and their personal belongings and you can hide here until we find something
better. There are no neighbors and no one can get up the
slope without being seen."

The house was a split-level stucco dwelling modestly
furnished with American sofas and carpets. Contemporary art prints hung on the walls and dust and cobwebs
were beginning to settle in the corners of the rooms.
Despite the distinctive and musty odor, the house was
an ideal hideout. It could only be reached by the driveway and directly in front of it was an open garden surrounded by large leafy trees with large yellow flowers.
The front windows were almost entirely overgrown with
lush green climbing plants and anyone approaching the
house could be discreetly observed.

Penina and I thanked Elijah for all his efforts and even
as we spoke there was the sound of a car in the drive.
Elijah quickly turned off the kitchen light and we huddled together on the floor by the window. Seconds later,
Ali's car appeared and we all breathed a sigh of relief.

Ali stayed only for a brief moment. He made certain
that we were safe and comfortable, and then he left to
visit the elders, house by house. He notified each one of
our whereabouts and for the rest of the evening there

was a steady stream of people passing through our hiding place. Each knock at the door brought a moment of intense anxiety and then a joyous, if sometimes fearful, reunion. Elijah's wife Maria arrived first and, when she told her sobering story, Penina and I realized for the first time the extent of our danger. Malire! A man who did not move, but gave orders! What could we have done to interest him? Was it because of the popularity of the church? The work of the orphanage? Many of the children now in the Kijomanyi Home were sons and daughters of prominent Ugandans killed by Amin, but was this enough to cause Malire himself to visit our home? It didn't seem likely that it was.

Kiwanuka arrived soon after Maria, bearing a cooked chicken in his hands, and I was almost smothered in his grand embrace. Tears ran down his cheeks and his joy empowered me to forget my fears. Kiwanuka began an up-to-date report on church affairs but before he could finish, Dr. K. and his wife arrived at the door. They too were carrying a chicken. Dr. K. was more tense than I had ever seen him, but his words were encouraging and he and Kiwanuka were soon laughing and joking together.

By midnight over a dozen elders had gathered and there were nearly as many chickens as people. Many of the men came with battered and disfigured faces. I found it difficult to look at them or to speak comforting words, but Kiwanuka immediately took things into hand. With his charming and imposing humor, he tried to make everyone forget their wounds.

"If we are wounded for Christ, Christ is the healer," he said, smiling broadly in his enthusiasm.

I worried that he was too loud for the thin walls of our hiding place, and I wondered if the elders resented his words because he had not suffered with them. Instead, they all nodded their heads in agreement. Each one seemed filled with peace and one young man spoke for them all. "Yes," he said, "and now, more than ever, we will serve Jesus Christ until the end comes."

At 1:00 Penina left with her cousin to visit her brother Godfrey. When she returned an hour later more elders had arrived. We sat together in the living room, listening to their experiences, and as each one shared about his time in the dungeons, one elderly man broke down in tears. He apologized to the rest of the elders, and then turned to me. The elders had agreed, it seemed, to say nothing of a deep disgrace they had experienced, but now he felt compelled to speak.

"When we went from church to the barracks," the elder said, "the soldiers ordered us to throw our Bibles in a pile. We obeyed, there was nothing else we could do. When all the Bibles were in one place, the soldiers gathered round them and urinated on them. The whole time they were laughing and using abusive language, and when they had finished, they were red-eyed and staggering. It was as if they had made themselves drunk.

"These men," the elder said, finishing his story, "drink a lot of gin to work themselves into a frenzy for killing. But after they had defiled the Word of God, they did not need to drink. And that's when they began beating us."

The story which the elders feared would discourage me lifted a great weight from my heart. Since our arrival at Entebbe Airport it had seemed to me that every single one of Amin's men was searching Uganda, hoping to destroy me and my family. Now I saw that it was not me who Amin was out to destroy. It was not the elders or the church. It was the Word of God. The soldiers had urinated on the Bible to remove from their lives God's restraining law.

I saw too that the elders had not suffered on my account. Only my own possessiveness could have made me think that. It was not *my* struggle, it was *our* struggle. And our struggle was for the sake of Jesus Christ. He had purchased us with His own blood and we were one with Him, and His sufferings.

Penina and I spoke with the elders for much of the night, catching up on news from the congregation and discussing the future of the church. The summer months were a time of rapid growth. A prominent government official had been converted, many sick and mentally disturbed people were being healed, and the all-night prayer meetings were now so crowded that dozens of people were forced to spend the night standing outside the building where the prayers were being held. At the same time, the number of people in need of counseling was increasing daily. There was no time to meet with them all, and there was no time for discipling new believers. The needs of our congregation had far outstripped our resources.

The future was a most pressing concern. Clearly, the Redeemed Church as we had known it had come to an end. After Sunday's raid it was unlikely that we could continue to hold public services. We would have to take the church underground. We would have to develop a network of invisible leadership and begin meeting again in individual homes. The project of breaking up our 14,000-member church in this way seemed to us an overwhelming task and out of fatigue and perhaps even fear, we all agreed that a discussion of a detailed plan should wait until the following evening.

Our meeting closed at 3:00 A.M. but many of the elders stayed for conversation and as we talked together, our thoughts turned naturally to the Resurrection. It was no longer a distant idea but a concrete reality, something so close that it gave power to our lives.

"It is because of the Resurrection that we are free," Kiwanuka said, speaking with a noble dignity. "We are not slaves to this life or to our fear of death. We are slaves to Jesus Christ and He has risen from the grave."

One of the elders who had been in Makindye Prison nodded his head. His face was covered with bruises and his nose was broken. "We are persecuted for the hope that is in us," he said. "Our hope is the Resurrection. We have nothing to worry about, Christ will fulfill our claims."

Several others spoke and then Dr. K., who had been strangely quiet the whole evening, leaned forward. He spoke in a low earnest voice and his spirit seemed far away.

"I have handled many dead bodies," he said. "And more come every day. *I am the resurrection and the life; he that believes in me, though he were dead, yet shall he live.* I tell you, a Man who says that, you need to listen to Him twice."

Towards morning, one by one, the elders said good-bye. Dr. K. was the first to leave and he spoke with deep feelings. We embraced and tears ran down our cheeks as we said good-bye.

The last to go was Kiwanuka. He grabbed both my arms in his large hands and seemed more confident and happier than ever. "You must know now," he said, "whatever comes, we are ready to die. For we are no longer following Kefa, we are following Jesus Christ."

With these words he stepped out the door. At the bottom of the steps he turned one last time before disappearing into the night.

"Good-bye, Kefa," he said quietly. "I will see you tomorrow."

For once in his life, Joseph Kiwanuka was wrong. We would not see each other on earth again.

It was early morning when Penina and I finally went to bed. We were too tired to sleep and as I lay awake in bed listening to the wind blow, my fears returned. Our hideout had been well-chosen but it was no fortress. Any curious passerby might be our undoing. And with hundreds of Amin's spies on the prowl throughout Kampala, it would be just a matter of days before we were discovered. Perhaps there was even someone in our own church community, someone eager to win a favor from the president's office. I looked at Damali, sound asleep at my side, and memories of the battered bodies I had seen in days past filled my head. *Maybe*, I thought, *my own child will soon be an orphan. . . .*

I jerked awake with a start. There had been a noise just outside the window, the sound of someone creeping along the wall. For a moment I was frozen in fear and then, because there was nothing else to do, I crept to the window. With my heart beating like a strained drum I peered furtively over the ledge. Everything was quiet. I sat in perplexed terror for several moments and then I heard the noise again. It was the sound of leaves rustling in the wind.

I went back to bed, trying to laugh, but I was still too afraid to sleep. *How often*, I asked myself, *had I stood in the church pulpit, six steps beyond the point of contradiction, and challenged the congregation to have faith in adversity? To trust in God's providential care?* Now it was my turn, not to preach but to believe, and I could hardly prevent my knees from shaking together. *Maybe*, I thought, consoling myself, *my heart is a believer and it is only my body that has no faith.* Even with this thought I knew that, in reality, the truth was more sobering. It was I, Kefa Sempangi, who with heart, soul and

150

mind was doubting God's Word and was without courage.

I fell asleep at dawn with a new understanding. My human weakness was no longer an abstraction to me; it was the concrete reality of my trembling body. "My grace is sufficient for thee: for my strength is made perfect in weakness."[19] The Word of the Lord to Paul was suddenly clear. It was not my own strength that would preserve me from death; it was the slain Lamb of God.

15

Standing in the Holy of Holies

Penina and I awakened late the next morning to a warm, cloudless tropical day. Red-tailed sunbirds with dark metallic wings and scarlet breasts were singing outside our window and the events and fears of the previous night seemed almost unreal. My sister, Nakazi, had spent the night on the living room couch and we could hear her now as she bustled around in the kitchen. The smell of curried chicken and *matooke* filled our bedroom. For the first time since our arrival, I felt hungry.

We sat down for lunch at noon and Nakazi reported on the news from my family. Things were beginning to go hard for those still in the village. The cash crop, coffee, was more and more confiscated by government soldiers and there was less and less hard currency for the purchase of staples like salt and sugar. My Aunt Lusi, who had put me through school with her 15 shillings, was in poor health, and my father was rapidly going blind. He was no longer able to work the long hours needed for subsistence farming and soon he would come to the city to live with his children.

The year before, my father had come to visit Penina and me in Kampala. One evening he startled us with the announcement that he had committed his life to Jesus Christ. "Not," my father had declared, "because of what men have said. Only because of what He has done. He is a God of power." I hoped that before long we would see him again.

After lunch my sister left with a woman from the church, Mrs. Okawa, to run some errands. The Okawa family was a family of wealthy merchants and Mr. Okawa was an influential member of the committee of elders. Both he and his wife were deeply concerned for the safety of my family and they were working closely with Ali to arrange a more permanent and secure hiding place.

Throughout the afternoon there was a steady stream of visitors and Penina and I passed our time in conversation with old friends. My mind frequently turned to the breakup of the church and by dinner time I had, I thought, a workable plan for organizing small underground households. In the light of day, such plans no longer seemed hopeless, and I looked forward to our meeting that evening with the elders.

At 6:00 we sat down to another chicken dinner. Just as we began to eat, the front door burst open. Mrs. Okawa rushed into the kitchen, followed closely by my sister. They were both out of breath and as Mrs. Okawa spoke, her words spilled out in our tribal tongue almost too quickly for us to understand.

"You must go!" she cried. "There's not a minute to lose. Someone has told the army of your hiding place and they know everything. They know all the places we have thought to hide you. You must leave Uganda now!"

Months later I learned that one of the committee of elders, a trusted friend of Penina's and mine, had betrayed us to his close friend, General Amin. But at that moment, with the arrival of the State Research Bureau just minutes away, there was no time for asking questions. Mrs. Okawa knew of a worker bus leaving Kampala for Nairobi, Kenya, at 6:15 and in seconds Penina and I decided that we would board it. We changed quickly into old clothes which we hoped would make us less conspicuous, and with trembling hands we packed our most important belongings into one suitcase. Then we grabbed Damali and ran outside to the drive where Elijah was waiting, once again, with a running car.

At the car door I said a tearful good-bye to my sister and as we embraced she whispered her sad news. "Last night, Kefa, Aunt Lusi passed away."

I hardly had time to understand her words. "We will miss you," I heard her say, and then we were inside the car and driving away.

The bus-park was only three miles away. We arrived at the station just as the worker bus was pulling away from the curb and as it slowed down to honk at a passing crowd of pedestrians, Elijah pulled alongside its front door. We jumped from the car, Mrs. Okawa shoved 600 shillings [20] into my hand, and before we could even think to say good-bye, we were inside the bus and headed down the road to Nairobi.

The bus was crowded with workers dressed in stained and ragged garments and there were no empty seats. We pushed our way in behind the driver and tried to ignore

154

his curious stares. No one was fooled by our old clothes and some of the seated passengers whispered among themselves of the curious event. The *abaana babowo*, members of the privileged class, were riding a bus with the poor.

Finally, after a brief stop just outside Kampala, two seats opened up in the back of the bus. Penina and I sat down with a sigh of relief on either side of a large, masculine-looking village woman. I was on the aisle, Penina and Damali were wedged firmly between the woman and two sleepy workers. Within minutes after we were seated the village woman who sat to my left began exerting steady pressure with her hips and shoulders to force me off the seat. I looked at her in surprise but she only stared straight ahead, her face set in a stony contempt, and pushed harder. She was a muscular woman in her late 50s and she was dressed in ragged clothes permanently stained by hard labor. Her curly hair was unkempt and she chewed her tobacco in a noisy, aggressive fashion. Beneath her feet, lying in a basket with their feet tied securely together, were three squirming chickens. Altogether, she seemed to me a formidable adversary and I found myself looking enviously at the people standing in the front of the bus. They, at least, were not afraid of suffering permanent damage to their hip bones!

For a long time it was all I could do to remain seated and I had no energy with which to worry about our dangerous situation. Finally, as I was about to fall into the aisle, the woman relented. I sat weakly back against the bench and closed my eyes in exhaustion. Sometime later I dozed off and almost immediately I was awakened by a painful pinch to the stomach. My eyes flew open and I found a hungry chicken sitting in my lap.

When the woman finally exited at a remote village

station my relief at her departure was undone by a sudden fear that she was one of Amin's killers in disguise. I expected her to board the bus again at any moment with a troop of soldiers. But we left the village without incident and we did not see the woman again.

It was midnight when we arrived at the Uganda-Kenya border. Both Penina and I had heard ugly rumors about soldiers at the crossing station—they raped women and arrested or killed men without the slightest provocation—but we were by then almost too tired to be afraid. An armed soldier boarded the bus through the front and ordered all the passengers to exit by the side door. Once outside we were divided into two groups, men to the right and women to the left, and marched to separate buildings for thorough searches.

I was about to enter a long, well-lit room where men undressed when a tall, ungainly Nubian grabbed me out of line. "You have money?" he asked. He spoke in a low voice and looked nervously over his shoulder.

I nodded and held up the 600 shillings I had received from Mrs. Okawa. The Nubian stared at the money in astonishment and then grabbed it out of my hand.

"You fool," he said, cursing loudly. "Don't you know that it's illegal to take more than 100 shillings across the border?"

It was a new regulation, established over the summer while we were in Holland. I was certain that the Nubian was going to have me arrested. Instead, he looked over his shoulder again, put 100 shillings back into my hand, and stuffed the rest of the money into his pocket. Then cursing with a loud voice to put on a good show for his fellow guards, he shoved me back to the bus. At the door, he gave me a sharp kick and as he pushed me inside the bus, he muttered under his breath, "You are a lucky man. You should be dead now!"

The border investigation took more than an hour and I waited anxiously for Penina and Damali. They were among the last to return. They themselves had not been ill-treated but Penina had seen others knocked around and abused. When the bus finally pulled away from the station, there were empty seats and missing faces to remind us of our narrow escape. We crossed over the border into Kenya, overwhelmed with relief and sadness.

We arrived in Nairobi in the early morning, completely exhausted, and spent the day trying to contact friends. My address book, which I thought was in a suit pocket, was missing and after an hour of searching for numbers in the public phone book, we set out on foot to visit the homes and offices of people we knew. We walked for miles, making dozens of stops. But everywhere we went, the story was the same: your friend has just moved, he is on vacation, he is studying abroad.

Towards evening we sat down on a park bench, too discouraged to walk another step. Our situation was beginning to seem desperate. We had been 24 hours without food or sleep and Damali, who until now had played happily in my arms, was exhausted and crying for food. We needed to find her something to eat and we needed to find a place to stay. It would not be wise to spend the night outdoors with a child.

We gathered up our strength and walked for another hour to the outskirts of Nairobi where lodging was cheap. After several false leads, we found a comfortable room for 90 shillings, bed and breakfast. We fed Damali sugar water and then, too tired to even plan for the morning, we collapsed into bed.

The next morning we woke early, packed our belongings, and went downstairs for breakfast. The dining room was a collection of rickety old tables behind the receptionist desk. As we drank our tea and ate our rolls we made our plans for the day. We would try again to contact a friend and hopefully, by nightfall, we would be settled.

I was just finishing my cup of tea when Penina grabbed my arm. I looked up and, over the receptionist desk, I saw a tall, muscular man with Nubian tribal scars walking through the door. He stopped at the desk to exchange a few words with the receptionist and then began thumbing through the guest book.

"Kefa Sempangi, what room is he?"

The manager said something inaudible and the Nubian headed up the stairs, two steps at a time.

By then my heart was in my throat. Penina and I got up from the table without speaking and, grabbing Damali and our suitcase, we walked out the back door of the hotel. Once outside, we began to run. We expected at any moment to hear pursuing footsteps and it was only when we were both out of breath that we slowed to a walk. A short time later we ducked into a doorway and, when we were able to speak again, we soberly considered our situation.

That Amin's Nubians should look for me in Nairobi came as a complete surprise. We knew that there were hundreds of Nubians in Nairobi and that the spy network of the State Research Bureau was extensive. We had heard, too, that Ugandans were sometimes kidnapped from Kenya and returned to Uganda for execution. But we assumed that these measures were only taken for prominent politicians; we never expected to face any danger ourselves once we were over the border.

"One thing is certain," Penina said. "If the State Research Bureau is still looking for you, it will not be long before they find you. We cannot hide forever in a country that is not our own."

I knew that what Penina said was true. The time had come to face the reality of our danger. We could no longer stay even in Nairobi.

I checked to make sure that we still had the "safety" air tickets which Mrs. Rookmaaker had so wisely provided, and I found them lodged securely inside my coat pocket. Our problem then became more immediate. With only 10 shillings left, we had no money with which to pay for a cab.

Across the street from where we stood was an attractive and motherly-looking woman standing next to a red sports car. The two of them, the car and the woman, seemed to me an unlikely pair and on a whim I suggested to Penina that we ask the woman for a ride. We crossed the street and found her to be extremely friendly. I explained to the woman that we didn't have any Kenyan currency to pay for cab fare and she laughed.

"I think you have no currency at all," she said. And then, so as not to give us false hope, "My husband never takes anyone in his car."

We continued to speak with her, and a few minutes later her husband walked up to the car. He greeted us in a hostile manner but after we spoke together briefly he shook our hands and commented that Damali looked very much like his own infant daughter.

"So," he said, "you need a ride. Get in. I will take you where you need to go."

On the way to the airport we learned that the woman was Lucy Ndibo. Her husband was the manager of Kimbo factory, a cooking oil company. They were extremely dignified and well-educated, and while they spoke with the authority of wealthy people, they were both dressed without ostentation. According to their own report, they had never known themselves to take in strangers from the street.

At the airport entrance, Penina and I said a grateful good-bye to the Ndibos and Mrs. Ndibo forced 10 shillings into my hand. "For the porter!" she said, waving aside my protest. She smiled and they both wished us good fortune as they drove away.

We walked into the airport and a porter grabbed our luggage. He stayed with us while we had our air tickets stamped and then walked with us to customs. At the gate I turned to give him his tip and he shook his head.

"No," he said, speaking in the tribal language of the Baganda. "I heard you and your wife speaking together. You are *wanainchi*, countrymen. You keep your money."

I insisted, but the porter shook his head.

"You keep your money," he repeated.

The next plane to London was leaving in 45 minutes but we cleared customs without any delay and headed towards the departure gate. Just as we were about to board the plane, we were stopped by an airline official.

"Your money, please," he said, holding out his hand.

We stared at him vacantly and he repeated his request.

"Your airline clearance tax. Didn't you read the sign?"

In our haste neither Penina nor I had noticed the signs posted around the airport informing passengers of an exit tax for anyone leaving the country. Now we looked at each other with dread, expecting the worst. I asked the man how much we owed.

"Each, 10 shillings."

Twenty shillings: 10 shillings left from Mrs. Okawa, 10 shillings from Mrs. Ndibo. I handed the money to the official with a gesture that implied there was plenty more where it came from, and Penina and Damali and I walked onto the plane.

160

We took seats towards the back and kept a careful watch on the front entrance, fearing at any moment to see a troop of armed Nubians storming down the aisle. But there was no further trouble. Before long the doors were sealed and we were taxiing down the runway for takeoff.

Once in the air, the numbness that had protected us since our escape from Uganda disappeared. Penina burst into tears and as I held her hand and tried to comfort her, I too was overwhelmed with grief. Nothing was left of the dreams we had brought to Uganda only a few days before. The Redeemed Church was broken up and the congregation scattered. The elders were in imminent danger. My Aunt Lusi was dead. We had left behind all our possessions—our house, our car, our furniture, the family photographs and heirlooms that were irreplaceable treasures. We owned nothing in the world now except the few items packed in one small suitcase beneath our feet.

Most frightening of all, we were no longer citizens of any country. There was no place on earth where we had civil rights, where we could claim the protection of the state. We could not go back to Uganda. We were heading to a foreign country for which we had no visas, no entrance papers and no money. What would happen to us? Where would we live and what would we do? How would I support my family? These questions caused me deep anxiety and I felt as if I would give anything for one more minute of prayer with the elders, one last chance for conversation.

Even with these thoughts I heard the voice of Dr. K. as he said good-bye on our last evening together. "The whole world might turn against you," he had reminded me, "but Jesus Christ stands with you."

Jesus Christ stands with you. These words penetrated

to my deepest fears. I shared them with Penina and we began speaking together of the remarkable way in which we had experienced God's presence since our arrival in Uganda. From our first step off the plane we were like sheep going to a slaughter. We walked into the hands of our enemies not once, but three times, and each time God redirected our footsteps towards His pastures. It was never a question of clever planning; from the beginning we were at our wits' end with no time or energy for strategizing. Now when we thought of Mrs. Ndibo's gift of 10 shillings and the porter's refusal to accept our tip, we were overwhelmed with awe. It seemed no matter what lay ahead, the worst was over. God had led us through the hurricane; He would see us through whatever storms remained.

We wanted to cry out on the plane, even as Dr. K. had one Sunday morning before the congregation: "Take off your shoes. You are standing in the holy of holies!"

16

Only Four Days Ago

"Wait aside, please."

We had just landed outside Amsterdam, in Schiphol International Airport, and we were standing in the exit line trying to explain our story to a customs officer. He was a large man dressed in a smart blue uniform and as soon as he discovered that we had no travel documents of any kind he waved us out of line. He spoke sharply in Dutch to a fellow employee and gestured in our direction. Moments later two more airline officials appeared and we were escorted down the corridor to a small room furnished only with a table and chairs. As soon as we were seated a policeman entered the room and the door was shut.

"Why did you leave Uganda without a visa?"

The officials asked the question repeatedly in a tone that suggested we were criminals. Each time Penina and

163

I told them the same story, and each time the officials stared at us skeptically and shook their heads. They had heard many wild stories from illegal immigrants; ours was not unusual. Hundreds of adventurous and discontented people from the Third World attempted to crash the borders of the western world every year. It was true that few could afford to fly as we had done; most came overland. But rules were rules. We could not stay in Holland.

As soon as Penina and I understood that the officials did not believe our story, and had no interest in anything we might say in our own defense, we asked them to call the Free University. They pushed our request aside with an impatient gesture and after asking a few more questions, they stepped outside for a private consultation. Minutes later they returned. Penina and I could read the bad news on their faces and we were not surprised when, motioning for us to get up, the chief official began ushering us out of the room.

"You cannot enter Holland without a visa," he said, taking us both by the arm. "We are putting you on the next plane for Uganda."

We found out later that it was cheaper for the airlines to put us back on the plane to Uganda than to pay the stiff fines exacted by the government for allowing passengers to board a plane without a visa.

At that moment, Penina and I felt as if the world was collapsing down around us. We stared at the officials in horror and in the most desperate language we pleaded with them to call the Free University. Again, they refused. The chief official seemed ready to evict us bodily from the room but just as he opened his mouth to speak, a government investigator walked through the door.

The investigator was a short stout man with a round

Dutch face. He inquired into the case with some thoroughness and listened carefully as the airline officials explained our story. When they were finished, the investigator turned to us with a sympathetic face. There was nothing he could do for us, he said, but he would "check out the facts." He would phone the Free University.

An hour later Dr. Rookmaaker walked into the room. He was followed by Dr. Van Noord, a high-ranking official from the Free University. To Penina and me, both men had the appearance of angels. But there was no time for joyous reunions. The airline officials, concerned that we might conspire together on a story, immediately ushered both men into a nearby office. The door closed behind them and once again Penina and I endured a long and anxious wait. By this time Damali had been without milk for two days, and she sat in Penina's lap and cried listlessly.

Behind the closed door Dr. Rookmaaker was presenting our defense to the government customs officials. He gave them clippings describing Amin's genocidal regime and produced one of the anonymous telegram we had received before our departure for Uganda. In the strongest of language he argued that Holland had always been, and ought still to be, a refuge for the oppressed.

"Uganda," he claimed, "is Hitler's Germany on a smaller scale. If you expel this family now, you will make us Dutchmen their murderers. Their blood will be on our hands."

After what seemed like hours, the office door opened and Dr. Rookmaaker and Dr. Van Noord walked out, followed closely by the airline officials and the government investigator. The investigator handed Penina and me several blank documents and a pen, and told us to write down our story in complete detail. When we finished we were given temporary identification papers and a stern warning to report to the local police in two weeks' time. A few minutes later, six hours after arriving in Amsterdam, we walked out of the airport. It was Thursday, September 20. With a start I realized that only four days ago we had left Amsterdam!

That night, thankful to be alive and too exhausted to worry about the future, we slept in an apartment furnished by the university. The following afternoon Nany Meister, a woman from the university foreign students office, offered us her apartment as a temporary home. Other friends joined quickly with Mrs. Rookmaaker and the orphanage organization, Stitching: Save a Child, to provide us with food and clothing. In two weeks we had everything we needed to make a home and Damali, who by then was in real need of stability, had settled down into a regular schedule.

In early October, just as we began to make plans for the future, our lives were once again disrupted. Penina went out one evening to a nearby department store to buy shoes for Damali, and while she stood in line at the cash register, a dark muscular man with Nubian tribal scars came walking through the door. He was wearing a flowered shirt and even through his dark glasses she could feel the intensity of his stare. He leaned against the wall with his hands in his pockets, and seemed to be waiting for Penina to make her purchase. Penina paid for the shoes with a shaking hand, and as she did, a cab driver rushed into the store. He caught sight of the Nubian and demanded in a loud voice that he either return to his cab or find a new one. The Nubian gave Penina one last look and walked out the door.

Penina came home that evening, trembling. She told me of her encounter and when she was finished we sat together for a long moment in shocked silence. The

166

weeks since we had fled Nairobi had already made the terror of Uganda seem a distant dream. We had never imagined that even in the bustling western metropolis of Amsterdam we would still be in danger.

It was true that we had heard stories. Only recently, the Ugandan ambassador to France had been assassinated outside his embassy in Paris. Around the same time, Scotland Yard reported that over 40 Nubian assassins were in England terrorizing Ugandan exiles. And in diplomatic circles, it was suspected that a general purge of Ugandan embassy personnel was on.

Penina and I had been alarmed by these reports but, since we ourselves were not involved with politics, we had not been afraid for our lives. Now suddenly, with the coming of the Nubian, our nightmare returned. It seemed there was no place on earth where we would be safe from Amin.

That night, before going to sleep, Penina and I read together from the Psalms. Since our escape from Uganda we had felt a deep kinship with David, the fugitive king. Now, more than ever, we were moved by his grief. We read from Psalm 18 and when we finished, Penina turned to me and said, "It is as if we are no longer reading the Psalms, but writing them—*The sorrows of death compassed me, and the floods of ungodly men made me afraid. The sorrows of hell compassed me about: the snares of death prevented me. In my distress I called upon the Lord, and cried unto my God: he heard my voice out of his temple, and my cry came before him, even into his ears.*"[21]

In the days immediately following Penina's encounter with the Nubian we spent most of our time in the apartment and went outdoors only to run errands or make trips to the university. The narrow streets of Amsterdam, which had once seemed so friendly and secure, were now sinister and oppressive. Often I found myself looking over my shoulder as if expecting at any moment to catch sight of a tall, shadowy figure trailing behind me.

This tension-filled existence might have continued indefinitely except for the assistance of the Rookmaakers. Early in November, thinking we would be safer in the countryside, they made arrangements for us to move to Eck en Wiel. We were given a room in the study center there and, when once again we were settled in, I went to work outdoors cutting trees. Before long, a tutor's position opened up in the study room. Grateful to be out of the northern winter, I moved indoors to supervise students and assist in the transcribing of tapes.

It was in Eck en Wiel that Penina and I made plans to go to America. The previous spring in the Rookmaaker's home, we had met Dr. Edmund Clowney, the president of Westminster Seminary in Philadelphia, Pennsylvania. Dr. Clowney and I spoke at length about the acute shortage of educated clergymen in Uganda and discussed the possibility of some elders from the Redeemed Church going to Westminster.

We soon discovered, however, that there was no one available who met the admission requirements. I was one of the few with a university background, and I had had no intention of leaving my teaching career.[22] Now, as a refugee with no career of any sort, my thoughts turned more and more to training for a future ministry among my people. At the recommendation of Dr. Rookmaaker, I wrote Dr. Clowney and requested admission to the seminary.

While waiting for Dr. Clowney's reply we received our first news from home—a letter from Ali. He was able to write only because he had left Uganda for a short vacation on the Mediterranean.

Brother Kefa, we must praise God for His
great works. You and your family crossed the
border into Kenya only minutes before the
news of your escape caused the closing of all
crossing stations. Amin's agents traced you to
Nairobi and then to the airport but when final-
ly they caught up with you, your flight was 30
minutes in the air.

Ali went on to give a complete report on the affairs
of the Redeemed Church. There were no longer any
public services held in the church compound; members
of the congregation were meeting in private homes for
worship. The elders had been threatened following our
escape but Kiwanuka had stepped over Malire and gone
straight to Amin himself to request that the elders be left
alone. No further trouble had come to them. On the
night we left Uganda, Malire and his men had invaded
the Kijomanyi Children's Home, but little damage had
been done and the home was still open. The only major
misfortune had befallen our own possessions. Our house
had been completely plundered and our car, a white
1971 Datsun, was now being driven around Kampala by
a well-known army captain.

News of the elders' safety brought fresh courage to
Penina and me, but our relief was short-lived. Within a
week after the arrival of Ali's letter we received a grim
update from Adoniya Kirinda, the elder of the Redeemed Church who had been directing the affairs of
the Kijomanyi Children's Home. Kirinda called from
London, where he had just barely escaped with his life.

"I returned home late one evening," Kirinda explained in a quiet voice, "and the body of my houseguest
was lying in a pool of blood outside the front door. He
was a new Christian and I was the one who led him to

169

Jesus Christ. His body had been run over by a truck and he had been shot many times at close range.

"I was afraid to go inside my house and I left immediately for a friend's home. From him I learned that soldiers had come to my home early in the evening looking for 'the man from the Kijomanyi Home.' They mistook my houseguest for me and when he protested, they dragged him outside and shot him. Then they left him bleeding to death in the dirt and piled into their trucks. As they drove away they ran over his body."

Kirinda was silent for a moment and then continued. He seemed deeply depressed and I did not know how to comfort him.

"I spent the night with my friend and then I went into the bush. After two days I crossed the border into Kenya. In Nairobi I heard that, after my disappearance, our brother M. was put in charge of the orphanage. But within a few days he too had to flee for his life. The Kijomanyi Children's Home has been disbanded and the orphans have been turned into the street."

This conversation with Kirinda left me feeling sick to my stomach. The faces of dozens of orphans passed through my mind and I imagined I heard them weeping on the streets of Kampala. Everything we had given to their lives was suddenly lost. How would they survive now? What about Okelo? He had lived in the security of the orphanage since his parents' killing and knew nothing of the animal existence of street children. Nothing in his wealthy upbringing had prepared him for a desperate fight for survival. And what about Florence and Topista? How long before, once again, they would be suffering from worms and malnutrition? How long before they forgot everything they had learned at school, before they joined the ranks of the hopelessly illiterate and became forever poor?

Kirinda's last remark to me on the phone only added to my discouragement. Kiwanuka himself was now in trouble. His most recent effort on behalf of the elders had angered Malire, and Malire swore to take revenge. It would be only a matter of time before he made good his promise. Kiwanuka stubbornly refused to believe he was in danger and firmly resisted all efforts to persuade him to leave the country.[23] But if he did not leave soon, his friends agreed, he would not leave at all.

Penina and I were deeply concerned for Kiwanuka and throughout November we prayed earnestly for his safety. Early in December we heard again from our friend in London. Kiwanuka's shop was surrounded one afternoon by Malire and his soldiers, but someone in the army had forewarned him of his danger. By the time the soldiers broke down the door, Kiwanuka was already on his way across the Kenya-Uganda border. Once in Kenya, he had been immediately welcomed into the most influential circles of Nairobi society. Kiwanuka had fought side-by-side with Jomo Kenyatta, the president of Kenya, during East Africa's struggle for independence. As a result he had many high-ranking friends in the Kenyan government, including Kenyatta himself. Now these friends promised to set him up with a new business and he was only waiting for his family to join him.

I was relieved to hear that Kiwanuka had finally left Uganda, but my family's own experience in Nairobi made me think he was not yet out of danger. I shared my fears with Mrs. Rookmaaker and Mrs. Rookmaaker, deeply concerned for Kiwanuka's safety, contacted the members of Stitching: Save a Child. Within days this small group of Christian believers found funds and sponsors to bring Kiwanuka to Amsterdam. Penina and I were overwhelmed by their unceasing generosity and

171

we immediately sent Kiwanuka a jubilant letter, inviting him to come to Holland. I told him of my plans to go to seminary and asked him to join me in training for the day when we would return to Uganda together, for the rebuilding of our country.

Kiwanuka did not answer my letter and I wrote him for the second time in mid-December. When I did not receive an immediate reply, I tried to track him by telephone through mutual friends in London. No one knew for certain where he was and, after several false leads, I came to a complete dead end. In utter frustration I wrote a third letter and prayed earnestly that the Kenyan postal authorities would finally deliver my message.

Two days before Christmas, while still waiting for Kiwanuka's reply, I received a letter from Leonidas Mukasa, an elder in the Redeemed Church. Mukasa, who had only recently escaped to London, wrote:

> *My dear brother Kefa,*
> *It is with deep regret that I inform you of the death of our beloved brother in Christ, Joseph Kiwanuka, who ten days ago was kidnapped from Kenya. He was taken by force back to Uganda, to Makindye Prison, and badly clubbed about the head by Malire and Amin. These men of Satan tried again and again to force him to renounce his faith but our brother lifted his hands to heaven and called the name of Jesus until his body collapsed dead.*

It was only later that I learned the details of Kiwanuka's death. He had been kidnapped from his hotel room in Nairobi by a gang of Nubians and taken directly to Makindye Prison. After being kept in a cell and tortured for several days, he was taken outside to the public yard, where both Amin and Malire were waiting with ham-

172

mers. Kiwanuka greeted them in a friendly fashion and, as their blows began to fall upon his body, he prayed aloud for the forgiveness of their sins. Amin went into an uncontrollable rage. Forgetting his desire to see his former friend die a slow and torturous death, he grabbed a nearby sledgehammer and slammed him over the head. Kiwanuka, with his last breath, called the name of Jesus and collapsed dead at Amin's feet. Amin then cut off his head and, after practicing blood rituals over Kiwanuka's remains, he stored his head in his freezer. He had been advised by his counselors, so the rumor went, that by preserving Kiwanuka's head he could make himself like "Jolly Joe, the smartest man in Uganda."

The news of Kiwanuka's death struck me as a physical blow. For days I was unable to eat or sleep. I did my duties in the study center as if walking in a dream and when I tried to pray, my prayers bounced off the ceiling. I no longer wanted to know God. How could He have taken Kiwanuka? How could I live and not see him again? Not hear his laugh or feel his strong embrace? I remembered Kiwanuka's tears from our last meeting and I thought of the many days we had spent praying and fasting for the ministry of the church. Now there was nothing left of the work we had done together. The church was scattered, the elders almost without exception were in exile, and the orphanage was destroyed. Everything was gone. I could not imagine beginning a new ministry without Kiwanuka and I no longer cared to ever see Uganda again.

My depression went on day after day and I became a stranger even to Penina and Damali. More than once the sound of laughter in the study room caused me to look up and stare at the door, as if at any instant I might see Kiwanuka walking through it. At such moments, and as if for the first time, I would feel again the pain of his death.

One afternoon, more than a week after receiving Mukasa's letter, I left my work in the study room and stole away to our bedroom to be alone. I lay down on the bed with an empty mind and tried to rest. A few minutes later, half-asleep and half-awake, I began to hear strange noises in the room. Suddenly, before my eyes, a crowd of people appeared. They were dressed in brightly-colored clothing and stood talking and laughing around tables piled high with food. The room was gaily decorated, as if for a party, and the sounds of merrymaking and singing filled my ears.

Just as suddenly the scene shifted. I saw before me a poorly-lit room crowded with men and women dressed in ragged, black mourning clothes. Their faces were contorted with grief. A small dog ran through the room chasing a miserable looking rodent and the sound of agonized wailing tortured my ears. In the midst of this dark confusion, I heard my own voice speaking.

"Where is God?" I asked accusingly. "Which room is He in?"

The mourners looked up startled and then stepped aside. For the first time I noticed a man and woman sitting in their midst, weeping. I drew closer to see them better and a shock of recognition passed through my body. It was Jesus at the grave of Lazarus, and He was weeping with Mary.

The vision faded and I found myself once again lying in bed. My head was spinning and I heard the words of Martha, as she stood outside the grave of Lazarus, ringing in my ears: "Lord, by this time he stinketh: for he hath been dead four days."[24]

For the first time I began to understand what it meant that Jesus Christ, the man of sorrows, had come to

174

where Lazarus lay stinking in his grave. He came to the hell of physical death and decay, where a man lay rotting, and He wept. Soon His own suffering would be upon Him; He would die on a bloody cross, tortured by the very people He came to save. His death would seem to be the last great triumph of Satan and his kingdom. But the foolishness of the cross, the concrete ugliness of a terrifying death, was "the power of God, and the wisdom of God."[25] Jesus Christ, the suffering Saviour of the world would enter the stinking grave, and as He raised Lazarus, He would raise His own children to everlasting life. "Christianity is resurrection," I heard Kiwanuka say. "We are no longer slaves to death."

With these words from Kiwanuka still ringing in my mind, my thoughts traveled back to a night late in 1972 when I had stood over the hospital bed of Samuel, a young man in our congregation. Samuel had been converted less than a year earlier from a life of street crime and, despite his youth, he became a zealous and wise believer. The previous night Samuel had attended an all-night prayer meeting, and we spoke together and read from the Psalms. Now he lay in a coma, his head swollen beyond recognition. Hours before he had been in a car accident and, as I looked down at his twisted body, I felt my heart fill with rage. I dropped to my knees and prayed beside Samuel's bed throughout the night.

"Oh God," I prayed, "Samuel cannot die. He is one of your children and you take care of your own. The doctors have given up hope, but you reach where man cannot reach. We have your promise, Jesus, that what is impossible for us, is possible for the Father, and if your words are not true, I do not know where else to go. Please save Samuel."

Samuel died at dawn. I sat by his bed and wept, and

then, sick with fatigue, I walked down the hospital corridor towards the door. As I passed through the waiting room I was stopped by a poor elderly woman who asked me if I was ill. I looked at her resentfully, but the humility and tenderness of her expression made me answer politely. I told her of Samuel's death.

"You know," she said, taking my arm, "through many losses of family and friends and through much sorrow, the Lord has taught me one thing. Jesus Christ did not come to take away our pain and suffering, but to share in it."

Now, almost a year later, the gentle words of the woman took on new meaning. I saw that in my grief over Kiwanuka's death I had come to think of myself as more reasonable than God, more compassionate. But God was not mourning for His people from a distance. His own Son had suffered the defeat of physical pain and death, and still suffered with the suffering of His children. We did not weep alone, Jesus Christ wept with us. And our sadness was only for a season:

> He that goeth forth and weepeth, bearing precious seed, shall doubtless come again with rejoicing, bringing his sheaves with him. [26]

What Kiwanuka and thousands of other martyrs had sown in tears, they, and the church with them, would reap in joy.

17

Our First Tomorrow

In February of 1974 Penina and I and Damali said good-bye to our friends in Holland and boarded a plane for the United States. We flew to Philadelphia, Pennsylvania and there, at Westminster Seminary, I began a three-year program of theological studies.

From our first week in Philadelphia we experienced again and again the openhearted generosity of American Christians. The seminary provided us with an apartment, and professors and their families contributed furniture. Our fellow students, some of whom barely had enough for their own families, gave us food and clothing, and a television set. Everywhere we went it seemed we had only to introduce ourselves, and exclamations of surprise would follow. "You are the Sempangis! Why, our family has been praying for you for months! Welcome to Philadelphia!" The warmth of these greetings made Penina and me feel immediately at home, and we felt a new sense of security and peace enter our lives.

Not long after our arrival, Penina announced one evening her plans for a shopping trip. There was a discount sale at a nearby department store and she wanted to buy while prices were low.

"Tomorrow," Penina said, "I'm going shopping at Sears for their big winter sale."

And then, before I could even respond, she burst into tears. I looked at her in alarm and, thinking she was worried about our finances, I assured her that we had money enough for her shopping trip. She only cried harder. A few moments later, she spoke through her tears.

"It isn't the money," she said. "Do you know that this is the first time in two years we have said 'tomorrow'?"

So that was it. Our first tomorrow. For two years we had lived in constant fear, unable to think of the future. All around us friends had disappeared, prominent citizens had been murdered, whole villages had been massacred. We never knew when our own time would come, and with bodies that shook at the sound of falling leaves, we had no energy to think of the future. Instead, like God's children in the wilderness, we learned to pray only for enough manna to get through the day. "Give us this day our daily bread." It was the prayer of a people who could not take God's grace for granted.

Penina went to the store the next morning just as she planned. In the days that followed, there were many more plans and many more "tomorrows." We learned to speak again of the future, and the tensions and anxieties that had become the norm for our existence disappeared. Even in Damali we could see a new calm and security.

Our first semester passed quickly. Penina gave birth to our son, Dawudi Babumba. In the fall I returned to my studies. It was then, in my second year, that I noticed the change that had come into my life. In Uganda, Penina and I read the Bible for hope and life. We read to hear God's promises, to hear His commands and obey them. There had been no time for argument and no time for religious discrepancies or doubts.

Now, in the security of a new life and with the reality of death fading from mind, I found myself reading Scripture to analyze texts and speculate about meaning. I came to enjoy abstract theological discussions with my fellow students and, while these discussions were intellectually refreshing, it wasn't long before our fellowship revolved around ideas rather than the work of God in our lives. It was not the blood of Jesus Christ that gave us unity, but our agreement on doctrinal issues. We came together not for confession and forgiveness but for debate.

The biggest change came to my prayer life. In Uganda I had prayed with a deep sense of urgency. I refused to leave my knees until I was certain I had been in the presence of the resurrected Christ. It was not just the gift I needed. I needed to see the Giver. I needed to know that the God of orphans and widows, the God of the helpless, heard my prayers. Now, after a year in Philadelphia, the urgency was gone. When I prayed publicly I was more concerned to be theologically correct than to be in God's presence. Even in private my prayers were no longer the helpless cries of a child. They were spiritual tranquilizers, thoughts that made no contact with anything outside themselves. More and more, I found myself coming to God with vague requests for gifts I did not expect.

One night, I said my prayers in a routine fashion and

179

was about to rise from my knees when I heard the convicting voice of the Holy Spirit.

"Kefa, who were you praying for? What is it you wanted? I used to hear the names of children in your prayers, the names of friends and relatives. You prayed for Okelo and Topista, for Dr. K. and Ali, for Nakazi and your father. Now you pray for 'the orphans,' for 'the church' and your 'fellow refugees.' Which refugees, Kefa? Which believers? Which orphans? Who are these people and what is it you want for them?"

It was a sharp rebuke. As I fell again to my knees and asked forgiveness for my sin of unbelief, I knew that it was not just my prayers that had suffered. It was not just a bad memory that caused names to vanish from my mind and turned those closest to me into abstractions. God Himself had become a distant figure. He had become a subject of debate, an abstract category. I no longer prayed to Him as a living Father but as an impersonal being who did not mind my inattention and unbelief.

From that night on, my prayers became specific. I prayed for real people, with real needs. And it was not long before, once again, these needs became the means by which I came face to face with the living God. In the spring of 1975 Penina and I received our first letter from the Ugandan refugee community in Nairobi. It was from Mrs. Ezeresi Kawooya, the widow in whose Kampala compound the Redeemed Church had met for worship, and the story she had to tell was sobering. Shortly after the death of Kiwanuka, Malire had begun making inquiries into her involvement with the Redeemed Church. In January of 1974, she was forced to flee Uganda with her four small children. They arrived in Nairobi without possessions or money, and slept on the street for days. Eventually Mrs. Kawooya found a small,

180

cheap room for rent and, by hiring herself out for cleaning and odd jobs, she was able to feed her family and keep them together.

Mrs. Kawooya had been in Nairobi only a few months when she began receiving visits from fellow refugees. By mid-1974 hundreds of Ugandans were fleeing their homeland every month, and night after night Mrs. Kawooya opened her door to the hungry and destitute. As long as there was space no one was ever turned away and as long as there was food no one ever went hungry. One morning, the irate landlord found 10 people sleeping in the room he had rented to five. He immediately threatened Mrs. Kawooya with eviction, and she promised to reform. Several mornings later, when the landlord returned, there were 12 people sleeping on the floor. They had come hungry and homeless, Mrs. Kawooya explained. How could she turn them away?

Now, she was in danger of losing her room. Her most regular cleaning job had ended, and none of her children had been able to attend school since their arrival in Kenya. She hoped soon to find a better job and when she did, she would enroll her two oldest children in a nearby primary school. That was the hardest part, her children were growing up without an education. Uganda refugee children are not allowed to attend government schools in Kenya and mothers often go hungry to provide their children with school fees. Having their children grow up without an education is one of the greatest frustrations refugees face, and it is especially difficult for those parents who themselves have received an education.

Penina and I read Mrs. Kawooya's letter with tears. We wanted desperately to send her money for the children, but we knew there was nothing we could do. We often joked to each other that the only thing in our refrigerator that never failed was the light and now, as

181

usual, we had just enough money for ourselves. There was no way we could help provide for someone else.

Several nights later, before going to bed, Penina and I had our devotions from Matthew 14. It was the same passage my brother from the Revival Fellowship had read to me so many years before. Jesus was in the desert, after the death of John the Baptist, and He commanded His disciples to feed the multitude. The disciples responded with incredulity. They did not have enough to feed themselves:

> *They said to him, "We have only five loaves here and two fish." And he said, "Bring them here to me." Then he ordered the crowds to sit down on the grass; and taking the five loaves and the two fish he looked up to heaven, and blessed, and broke and gave the loaves to the disciples, and the disciples gave them to the crowds. And they all ate and were satisfied.* [27]

Penina and I read these words aloud and then sat in silent amazement as a new understanding came to our hearts. In the breaking of the bread, Jesus showed His disciples God's own response to persecution. John the Baptist had been martyred, but in the midst of His grief Jesus humbled Himself to serve the Father. He fed a hungry people with bread and pointed to His own death on the cross. "Take, eat: this is my body broken for you,"[28] Jesus would say. God had sent His only Son to be blessed and broken, to be given in the midst of betrayal and death for the salvation of His people. Likewise, Jesus was calling His disciples to participate in His suffering. He was calling them to obedience.

That night Penina and I realized that we too had been called to a ministry of obedience. We could not stand at a distance and say to our fellow refugees, "Our hearts are broken by your suffering." Only as we shared in their suffering by sharing our possessions would our hearts truly be said to be broken. But Jesus was not commanding us to feed His sheep from our own sufficiency. He was not concerned about the size of our bank account. He was only asking that we bring the little that we had to Him. He would bless it and break it and use it in the midst of persecution to feed His children.

"I think there is something we can send to Mrs. Kawooya," Penina said, when we finished talking that evening. "We can send her the 20 dollars in my purse."

Under the shadow of Mrs. Kawooya's needs, 20 dollars seemed more like nothing at all; but the next morning, after asking God to bless and multiply our gift, we sent the money on to Nairobi. We explained to Mrs. Kawooya that we would send more as soon as we could, and asked her not to give anyone in Nairobi our address. We did not want to be flooded with requests for money and we still had some concern for our safety.

In three weeks time, we began receiving letters from Nairobi. "A secret friend" had given our name, could we help a homeless family of eight? "A respectable lady" had said we might offer assistance, did we have money for children's school fees? Could we help pay a large hospital bill? Would we sponsor a university student in his last year of medical school?

Penina and I read these requests and did not know whether to laugh or cry. Our own finances were tighter than ever. We had no more money for Mrs. Kawooya, how could we help the total strangers she sent to our door? Without loaves, what was there to multiply? In deep frustration, we spent long nights in prayer asking God to meet the needs of those who had turned to us for help.

Within the same month, an anonymous donor sent

Penina and me a check for 800 dollars. The money came through the seminary and when Penina and I heard the news we stared at each other in disbelief. We had not expected so much from our prayers. We only thought that someday soon we would have another 20 dollars to spare. Now, suddenly, we had 40 times that much.

Just as suddenly, we found ourselves overcome by a spirit of possessiveness. Twenty dollars was easy to surrender; 800 dollars could buy a car or furniture for the apartment. We could get a washer and dryer, and a new bed for the children. Surely God would want us to take care of ourselves! After all, the money had been sent to *us*. We could meet our own needs and still have money left to send a generous gift to Mrs. Kawooya.

Even as we rationalized, the Spirit of Christ moved us to obedience. We knew the money had come in answer to our prayers for the refugees; we knew the money belonged to them. It was not ours to keep, but to pass on. We sent the 800 dollars to Mrs. Kawooya and asked her to distribute the money among those refugees who had written to us for help. And we made a new promise to God: whatever He put into our hands with the command to distribute, whether it was 50 cents or a million dollars, we would not keep to ourselves. We would pass it on to His children.

From this time onward a steady stream of funds passed through our hands. Friends from the seminary began giving us money designated for our fellow refugees and soon area Sunday School classes and Bible studies were taking up special collections. More and more I found myself speaking in front of churches and clubs about the needs of Ugandans in Nairobi.

In the three years since my family and I had escaped from Uganda the number of our countrymen living in exile had grown from a mere handful of political refugees to over 100,000 men, women and children. Those forced to flee were largely professionals—lawyers, doctors, agriculturalists, educators, businessmen and top-level military personnel—and they and their families seldom arrived in Kenya with more than the clothes on their backs. For the many who could not afford to move on to the West, life immediately became a tremendous fight for survival. Unemployment among Kenyans stood at 60 percent and the Kenyan government passed strict laws forbidding refugees to work.

As a result of these laws, thousands of Ugandan families were living in the most desperate conditions. They slept in parks, or crowded into garages and servants' quarters, and at times were forced to beg for food. A constant flow of Amin's spies in and out of Kenya created an atmosphere of tension and suspicion, and it was not unusual for Ugandan refugees to disappear. Of all these hardships, perhaps enforced idleness was the worst. Men who had trained for years to practice professional skills suddenly found themselves with nothing to do—all day long.

Word spread quickly among these desperate exiles that help might be available from the United States and soon a steady stream of letters from Nairobi began arriving at our door. Many were written by those who had only recently escaped from Uganda and the news they brought from home was devastating. The Israelis' successful "raid on Entebbe" in July of 1976 had brought deep humiliation to Amin. As he fought desperately to regain his authority, thousands of Ugandans were killed. There was renewed persecution of Christians, and a raid on Makerere University left the school temporarily closed and hundreds of students dead. In October, even two of Amin's own sons were sent to prison.

Uganda itself was bankrupt. Amin's "economic war"

had failed and the Uganda shilling was worth only 10 percent of its former value. Were it not for subsistence farming, millions of Ugandans would have been starving to death. To get basic commodities like salt and sugar, men and women were forced to stand in long lines at government stores, knowing that even after hours of waiting they might get nothing at all. In one sugar line, a recent refugee wrote, there was a woman with a starving child. She had sold everything she owned to come to the city and buy food. As she stood with her child in anxious desperation at the end of the line, a sympathetic man standing behind her suggested she ask someone at the head of the line for a place. The woman moved forward and a mercenary guarding the line came to see what she was doing. He spoke a language she did not understand, and when she stumbled, he kicked her to the ground. The soldier continued to kick the woman until she died, still clutching her dying child. No one turned to protest. The defenseless men and women thronged on to get their sugar, and the mercenary dragged the woman across the way and dumped her body in the bush.

For every letter like this one, with a story of suffering and terror, there was another letter that spoke of God's grace and incomprehensible love. These testimonies often caused Penina and me to weep, and for the first time we began to catch glimpses of meaning in the otherwise senseless destruction of our country. One exiled member of the Redeemed Church wrote:

> *Praise God for the testimony of Jesus Christ who even in death brings life and hope! Praise God for the testimony of Major Emmanuel Ogwal! Major Ogwal was an Obote supporter who preached his first and last sermon from*

the edge of the grave. One day he was chased through the center of Kampala by Amin's soldiers and when he tried to hide in the house of Dr. George Ebine,[29] there was a long shoot-out. Afterwards, Major Ogwal was found mortally wounded and praying to God. One of the soldiers held a knife to the Major's throat and, cursing, threatened to cut off his head unless he stopped praying. The Major looked him in the eye, with blood streaming down his face. "I am praying for you," he said. There was another violent threat, but Major Ogwal kept on praying. The soldier cut off his head. Major Ogwal's life on earth ended but one of the soldiers participating in his murder was moved to repentance by the testimony of his death. Later, the soldier found a pastor and confessed his sins and became a follower of Jesus Christ.

Mrs. Florence Lubega, a former member of Uganda's parliament, also sent a letter. Her husband had recently been murdered, and she wrote from London, where she was living in exile:

Ever since my conversion, I have been praying that God would dispose of Amin. I have wished him dead and when I see his picture in the news I feel sick. Now, I don't know how to pray. After fleeing from Uganda I had nothing. Everything I owned was taken by Amin's soldiers. I lived in Nairobi for almost a year, and I slept in a garage with only newspapers between my body and the cold cement floor. I had nothing to eat. It was then I learned what I had not learned sleeping on a mattress with

187

a full stomach. I learned to love Jesus Christ, the suffering Saviour. Since then, I have come to London and still have been praying for the death of Amin. But should I instead be praising God for raising a man so evil that he took everything I owned and caused me to see the Lord? "In the year that King Uzziah died I also saw the Lord" (Isaiah 6:1). It is when everything is uncertain that God's face becomes clear.

Mrs. Lubega's letter brought new healing to my life. I too had come to hate Amin and I too felt sick at the sight of his face. The thought of the thousands of defenseless people he had slaughtered made me long for his death. But Mrs. Lubega was right. Amin himself stood defenseless before the grace of God, and he could not escape. He had chosen the weapons of suffering and terror to destroy God's people, but God had taken those weapons and used them to redeem His children.

From Mrs. Lubega's letter, and from hundreds of others like it, Penina and I learned an important lesson. The story of what God was doing in Uganda did not end with Idi Amin. What Pharaoh had meant for evil, God was using for good. For every newspaper headline, for every story of atrocities and death, there was another story which went unreported and unnoticed. It was the story of those who, by faith, had "escaped the edge of the sword" and those who, by faith, "were slain with the sword."[30] It was the story of how God's people, in the midst of great suffering, had come to understand the depths of love. And it was the story of how God, in His providence, had led His children into the wilderness, to prepare a table before them.

When they are diminished and brought low

through oppression, trouble, and sorrow, he pours contempt upon princes and makes them wander in trackless wastes; but he raises up the needy out of affliction, and makes their families like flocks. The upright see it and are glad; and all wickedness stops its mouth. Whoever is wise, let him give heed to these things; let men consider the steadfast love of the Lord. [31]

Editor's Postscript

The ministry to Ugandan refugees which began in the Sempangi's home in Philadelphia soon expanded. In 1976, with the help of men like John Perkins, Robert DeMoss and Jack Miller, the first fund for refugees was officially established.

The relief efforts of those involved with the Africa Foundation Inc. are concentrated in Nairobi, Kenya, where three staff members are presently living. The short-range plan of the Africa Foundation Inc. team, which now consists of eight members, is to provide refugees with self-help projects, discipleship counseling and student scholarships. Their long-range plan is to train Christian men and women to take part in the rehabilitation and development of Uganda once justice is restored to that country.

Further inquiries about the Africa Foundation Inc. and its ministry may be directed to:

F. Kefa Sempangi, Director
Africa Foundation Inc.
Box 1806 College Station
Fredericksburg, Virginia 22401

Notes

1. Hal Sheets, *New York Times.*
2. The East African Revival was begun in 1930 and has lasted until the present time. The word "revival" is understood in East Africa in a different sense than it is in the western world. It is not mass evangelism, but an internal conviction of sin within a fellowship group that leads the group to confession. The word used is *okulongosa* which, translated literally, means "a cleaning up." It is what happens when light breaks into a community of believers and humbles them for repentance and forgiveness.
3. *Kijomanyi* is taken from a Ugandan proverb similar to the English proverb "A stitch in time saves nine." Kijomanyi (pronounced Kē jō man gē) means "he who heeds a first warning does not lose the harvest."
4. John Taylor, *The Growth of the Church in Baganda* (London: SCM Press, Ltd., 1958).
5. Matthew 5:23,24.
6. See John 15:15.
7. Matthew 14:19, *RSV.*
8. Luke 5:8.
9. Luke 11:20.
10. These are the words of the Libyan delegate who presented the money to the Ugandan Muslim Supreme Council. This information as well as information concerning Amin's "list of 2,000" was first circulated in a top secret memo by E.B. Rugamayo, former minister of education in Uganda. His testimony has since been published by the International Commission of Jurists in Uganda and Human Rights, "Reports to the UN Commission on Human Rights," 1977.
11. See John 15:5; 14:10.
12. The name has been altered to protect the lives of those still living in Uganda.

13. Luke 2:29-41.
14. See Galatians 2:20.
15. Isaiah 44:22.
16. See Revelation 12:11.
17. Several names and minor details of events described in this chapter have been changed to protect the lives of those still living in Uganda.
18. Makindye Prison, nicknamed "Singapore" after the Malaysian capital Obote was visiting the night he was overthrown, is one of three notorious prisons run by Amin's regime. At any time of day one can hear the inhuman groans and screams of its inmates. Not long ago it was reported that the blood in its cells was over a half-inch thick. Makindye was first known for its brutal treatment of political prisoners. In September of 1972, Joseph Wacholi, a cabinet minister under Obote, had his head split open in the courtyard by a military policeman. Since then passersby and wardens have reported all kinds of terrible tortures taking place in full view of the public. So that prisoners cannot escape, the guards cut off their arms or legs, or remove their eyes. And when they have finished with their tortures, they either behead their victims or cut them to death by inches.
19. 2 Corinthians 12:9.
20. The shilling, in September of 1973, was worth 20 cents. One year later it was worth only 16 cents and the Ugandan economy was on its way to an inflation rate of 500 percent.
21. Psalm 18:4-6.
22. When Dr. Clowney first suggested to me that I consider coming to Westminster Seminary, both Penina and I had stared at him strangely. Despite our years of working with missionaries, neither of us had ever heard the word "seminary." The only word we knew was *seminario*, a Catholic monastery. We were surprised, to say the least, that Dr. Clowney could suggest the monastic life for a married man.
23. This resistance to flight, well-known to those living under tyrannical regimes and almost incomprehensible to those living in the comfort and security of democracy, was explained by Alexander Solzhenitsyn in *The Gulag Archipelago*. Solzhenitsyn, commenting on his countrymen's passivity in the face of Stalin's slaughters, says: "Universal innocence also gave rise to the universal failure to act. Maybe they *won't take* you? Maybe it will all blow over? . . . Since you aren't guilty, then how can they arrest you? *It's a mistake*. They are already dragging you along by the collar, and you will keep on explaining to yourself: 'It's a mistake! They'll set things straight and let me out!' " (New York: Harper and Row Publishers, 1973), p. 12, I-II.
24. John 11:39.
25. 1 Corinthians 1:24.
26. Psalm 126:6.
27. Matthew 14:17-20, *RSV*.
28. See 1 Corinthians 11:24.
29. Dr. Ebine knew nothing of Major Ogwal's attempt to hide in his home, but a short while later the soldiers traced him to his hospital and arrested him in the operating room. He was taken to Makindye Prison where he was crushed to death by a tank.
30. Hebrews 11:34,37.
31. Psalm 107:39-43, *RSV*.